ECONOMIC ANALYSIS OF
ENVIRONMENTAL PROBLEMS

ECONOMIC ANALYSIS OF
ENVIRONMENTAL PROBLEMS

Gregory C Chow
Princeton University, USA

World Scientific

NEW JERSEY · LONDON · SINGAPORE · BEIJING · SHANGHAI · HONG KONG · TAIPEI · CHENNAI

Published by

World Scientific Publishing Co. Pte. Ltd.

5 Toh Tuck Link, Singapore 596224

USA office: 27 Warren Street, Suite 401-402, Hackensack, NJ 07601

UK office: 57 Shelton Street, Covent Garden, London WC2H 9HE

Library of Congress Cataloging-in-Publication Data
Chow, Gregory C., 1929–
  Economic analysis of environmental problems / Gregory C. Chow.
    pages cm
  Includes bibliographical references and index.
  ISBN 978-9814390392 (alk. paper)
  1. Environmental economics. 2. Environmental policy--Economic aspects. I. Title.
HC79.E5C492 2015
333.7--dc23

                                                        2014031032

British Library Cataloguing-in-Publication Data
A catalogue record for this book is available from the British Library.

Typeset by Stallion Press
Email: enquiries@stallionpress.com

Printed in Singapore

To Paula

Preface

There is an extensive literature on the economics of environmental problems. The purpose of this book is to introduce and apply the method of dynamic economics to study a selected set of such problems. The important variable in these problems is the quantity of pollution or carbon emission. A utility function of the quantities of consumption and emission is maximized in the static (one period) and dynamic (multi-period) settings. The optimum amounts of consumption, emission and other economic variables are found. This method emphasizes the cost of reducing emission and the tradeoff between emission and other important economic variables since the reduction of consumption or output is required for the reduction of harmful emission given the state of technology. The case of several economies is also included. Models to study the control of carbon emission in the world are presented. Environmental policies are studied from the theoretical, empirical and institutional points of view.

Chapter 1 provides an introduction to our general approach and includes the formulation of a number of utility maximization problems. Chapter 2 provides an institutional setting by discussing China's environmental problems and policies. In Chapter 3, a dynamic optimization problem is formulated to study the optimum path for the control of carbon emission in the world and the problem is solved numerically. In Chapter 4, two macro-economic models incorporating the consideration of the environment in the utility function will be presented and estimated using Chinese data. The first model uses the same utility function as in Chapter 1 while the second model uses a different utility function which includes cumulative emission E as an argument. In addition, the second model treats emission e as a factor of production. In Chapter 5, stochastic models are presented to study the effect of climate change while Chapter 6 introduces parameter uncertainty in models of global warming. In Chapter 7, we formulate models of dynamic games to study regional differences in environmental policies by postulating different utility functions for different regions. Chapter 8 presents two macroeconomic models to explain pollution and other important macroeconomic variables. The first model has the same utility function as the first model of Chapter 1 but treats emission as a factor of production. The second model of Chapter 8 adds scrubbing as an additional control variable to the first model. The use of emission permits as a means for environment protection is discussed in Chapter 9. Chapter 10 presents empirical studies of the environmental Kuznets curve. Chapter 11 presents different ways to produce clean energy and discusses possible institutional arrangements in the world to control climate change.

This book is written for advanced undergraduates and graduate students in economics and other disciplines. The exposition is self-contained. The prerequisites are multivariate calculus, matrix algebra and mathematical statistics. The book is not a comprehensive treatment of the subject. It is rather a presentation of a selected set of models to study environmental problems using the method of dynamic economics.

The material of this book was used in a graduate seminar in the Department of Operations Research and Financial Engineering of the School of Engineering and Applied Science at Princeton University and in a course in the Department of Economics at the Hong Kong University of Science and Technology. Faculty members at Princeton participated in teaching the seminar and helped me learn much of the subject. I would like to acknowledge critical comments on my lectures from students at both universities. Ning Lin at Princeton provided valuable comments on parts of the book manuscript. Especially I would like to thank Fuhai Hong at Nanyang Technological University for going through the entire book and correcting many errors. Lixi Dong of World Scientific Publishing Company offered invaluable assistance in editing this book. Financial support from the Gregory C Chow Econometric Research Program is gratefully acknowledged.

Gregory C Chow

Princeton, NJ

August 23, 2014.

―――

About the Author

Gregory C Chow is Professor of Economics and Class of 1913 Professor of Political Economy, Emeritus, at Princeton University. He has made important contributions to econometrics (including the famous Chow test), applied micro and macroeconomics, dynamic economics and the Chinese economy. Upon his retirement from Princeton University in 2001, the Econometric Research Program was renamed the Gregory C Chow Econometric Research Program in his honour.

He is a member of the American Philosophical Society and Academia Sinica in Taiwan, a Distinguished Fellow of the American Economic Association, a Fellow of the Econometric Society and the American Statistical Association. His publications include 17 books and over 200 articles. The books include: *Demand for Automobiles in the United State: A Study in Consumer Durables* (North Holland Publishing Company, 1957); *Analysis and Control of Dynamic Economic Systems* (John Wiley & Sons, 1975); *Econometrics* (McGraw-Hill Book Company, 1983); *The Chinese Economy* (Harper & Row, 1985); *Understanding China's Economy* (World Scientific, 1994); *Dynamic Economics: Optimization by the Lagrange Method* (Oxford University Press, 1997); *Knowing China* (World Scientific, 2004), *Interpreting China's Economy* (World Scientific, 2010), *China as a Leader of the World Economy* (World Scientific, 2012); *China's Economic and Social Problems* (World Scientific, 2014); *Routledge Handbook of the Chinese Economy* (Routledge, 2014); *China's Economic Transformation* (Wiley, 2015, forthcoming).

Professor Chow served as Chairman of the American Economic Association's Committee on Exchanges in Economics with the People's Republic of China from 1981 to 1994 and as Co-chairman of the US Committee on Economics Education and Research in China with support from the Ford Foundation from 1985 to 1994. He was a member of the US-Hong Kong Economic Cooperation Committee. He advised former Prime Ministers and Chairmen of the Economic Planning and Development Council of the Executive Yuan in Taiwan on economic policy from the mid 1960s to the early 1980s. Under the sponsorship of the Chinese State Education Commission (now Ministry of Education), he was responsible for a one-year program in Renmin University of China (1985--1996) and in Fudan University (1988-1993) to teach modern economics in China and for a special program to place graduate students from China to pursue a PhD degree in top universities in the US and Canada. He has advised the Prime Minister and the State Commission for Restructuring the Economic System on economic reform in China. He has been appointed Honorary Professor at Fudan, Shandong, Hainan, Nankai, Huazhong Science and Technology, Guangxi and Sun Yat-sen Universities, Renmin University of China and the Chinese Academy of Sciences; Honorary President and Honorary Chairman of the Board of Trustees of Lingnan (University) College; member of the Advisory Board of Directors of Sun Yat-sen University. He received an Honorary Doctor's Degree from Sun Yat-sen University in 1986, an LL.D. from Lingnan University in Hong Kong in 1994 and an Honorary Doctor of Business Administration from the Hong Kong University of Science and Technology in 2009. He is an independent director of the Taiwan Semiconductor Manufacturing Company and writes a column for *China Business News* (Diyi Caijing Ribao), *Southern Metropolitan News* (Nanfang Dushi Bao), *Financial Times*, Chinese edition, in China and *Commercial Times* in Taiwan.

Contents

Preface   vii

About the Author   xi

1. Environmental Economics: Basic Ideas
   and Analytical Methods   1

2. China's Energy and Environmental Problems
   and Policies   17

3. Optimal Path for CO_2 Emission to Control
   Global Warming   41

4. Macroeconomic Models Incorporating
   the Effect of Pollution   61

5. Stochastic Models to Study the Effect
   of Climate Change   87

6. Parameter Uncertainty in Models of Global Warming   103

7. Regional Differences in Environmental Policies   117

8. Macroeconomic Models to Explain Pollution
   and Environmental Protection   133

9. Use of Emission Permits   143

10. Environmental Kuznets Curve   159

11. Clean Energy and International Efforts to Solve
    Environmental Problems   169

Index   187

Chapter 1

Environmental Economics: Basic Ideas and Analytical Methods

1.1. Introduction

This book is concerned with the problem of environmental degradation in the course of economic development, a topic that has attracted much attention in recent years. See Maler and Vincent (2005), for example. Because there are many important aspects of environmental problems and many interesting questions that can be raised, different models have been proposed. For example, Nordhaus and Boyer (2000) presented a large economic model to assess the effects of different policies to mitigate the harmful effects of climate change. Stern (2007) conducted a comprehensive study of both the analytical and policy aspects of climate change. Andreoni and Levison (2001) provided a model to explain the environmental Kuznets curve, namely, pollution first increasing and then decreasing in the course of economic development. The models of this book will address some basic issues of environmental pollution and degradation based on the idea that the natural resources available in the environment are underpriced, leading to economic inefficiency and wastes.

A main body of economics is concerned with efficient allocation of resources given the state of technology. By an efficient allocation of resources, it is meant that the economic resources are used to produce the maximum amounts of goods and services, in the sense that more of one good or service cannot be produced without sacrificing the output of another. Since the same economic resource can be used to produce different outputs, the most basic principle under the efficient allocation of resource is that each resource should contribute an additional output (its "marginal product" in the terminology of economics) of the same value, no matter which output

1

is under production. Otherwise, moving the resource from a less to a more productive use will increase the total value of all outputs. Adam Smith (2009; first published in 1776) has pointed out that an efficient allocation of resources in the sense defined above can be achieved in a market economy by allowing the consumers to purchase what they desire and the producers to produce what is most profitable. Under suitable conditions, decentralized decisions made by many consumers and producers separately, without government intervention, can maximize economic welfare, as if these decisions were guided by an "invisible hand". Modern economists have refined this important idea by specifying precisely mathematical conditions and providing rigorous proofs of this proposition.

Environmental economics deals with an important situation, where the market or the working of the invisible hand may fail. The environment is treated as a natural resource or natural capital, in the same way physical capital and labor are treated as factors of production, an approach first taken by Brock (1973). This resource was not treated explicitly in the study of economics because it was so plentiful. When an unlimited amount of a resource is available, there is no problem in allocating it efficiently for alternative uses. Using it to produce one commodity will not affect its use for producing another commodity, since the supply is unlimited. In the course of rapid economic development, however, natural resources like clean air and usable water have been used so extensively that they have become limited in supply and the quality of the resource is affected. This gives rise to an important field of environmental economics that deals explicitly with the efficient use of natural resources. Environmental economics treats natural resources explicitly and suggests ways to use them efficiently. A key question is how to put these natural resources to their most efficient use such that it results in as much utility or welfare for the society as possible.

In an efficient allocation of a natural resource, we consider the tradeoff between its alternative uses. This means to compare the harm or disutility of pollution that results from using a natural capital and the benefit of its use in the production of more output. Consider a classic example of the production of steel by a factory that emits soot in the air. There is a tradeoff between the output of steel and the amount of polluted air. The optimum amount of air pollution is not zero, because if no polluted air is allowed, no steel can be produced given the technology. An optimum amount of air pollution in this case strikes a balance between having more output of steel and having more clean air.

In this chapter, I will provide simple economic models in which balancing the costs and benefits from the use of natural capital is required. I will start with a simple case in Section 1.2, where there is only one variable to measure the amount of pollution or emission of pollutants in the use of natural capital, and the optimum amount will be determined by the government or a central planner having full knowledge of the economy. Section 1.3 shows that, if the government does not have complete knowledge of the parameters describing the economy, but the consumers have property rights to natural capital and can sell emission permits to the producers, the market solution will yield the same optimum that a government having complete knowledge of the economy can achieve. In the market solution, pollution permits are supplied by the consumers who have property rights to the environment and demanded by producers who are required to have the permits for production. In Section 1.4, I will discuss briefly the problems in the implementation of an optimum amount of pollution that is determined by the government or by the market forces of demand and supply.

Section 1.5 deals with the case of two economies sharing the same natural resource. The action of one economy in setting the amount of pollution affects the action of the other. Theory of games is applied to find solutions for the two economies. Section 1.6 studies the dynamic case for one economy when its consumers and producers have utility and profit functions in the consumption and production over many periods. The objective is to find an optimum time path of emission. Section 1.7, like Section 1.5, allows two economies to share the same natural capital and determines the optimal time paths of emission for both economies in a dynamic game.

This book brings together useful ideas and tools in economics in order to understand environmental problems and to provide solutions to them. By a solution I mean not only finding the optimum amount of pollution based on an economic model but also suggesting ways to implement the solution in practice and dealing with practical difficulties in implementation of environmental policies. An example can be found in Section 1.4 and will be discussed in more details in Chapter 2, when China's environmental problems and policies are addressed. In Chapter 2, I present two proposals for improving the protection of China's environment, one including a practical way to find the optimum amount of pollution to be enforced.

1.2.   A Simple Model of Pollution

To illustrate how the cost and benefit of pollution is balanced, let us assume the consumers of an economy to have the utility function:

$$\log c + \theta \log(M - e), \tag{1.1}$$

where c denotes the amount of consumption, e denotes the amount of emission of pollutants and M is an amount somewhat larger than the maximum tolerable amount of emission for human survival. If M is just equal to the maximum tolerable amount, when e is close to that amount, or $M - e$ is close to zero, $\log(M - e)$ will tend toward negative infinity and the second term dominates the first term in the above utility function. When this happens, too much weight will be given to the second term of the utility function (1.1) as compared with the first term. In this utility function, a large value for θ means that having a cleaner environment matters a great deal as compared with having more consumption goods. The larger the value of e, the more polluted is the environment and smaller the utility. Given θ, a larger value of M reduces the importance of pollution in the utility function. The reason is that when M is large, a given change in e will mean a smaller percentage change in $M - e$. Our utility function measures the effect of $M - e$ on utility in percentage terms by using its natural logarithm.

For the purpose of illustrating the basic principles involved, I assume a Cobb-Douglas production function when treating e as a factor of production together with the other two factors capital K and labor L. I assume that consumption equals output in this model and that output equals Ae^{δ} where A is a function of K and L and is treated as a constant for the purpose of the present discussion, because we are holding K and L constant. A larger e will allow more output in the first term $\log(Ae^\delta)$ of (1.1) while it creates disutility from the second term.

The benefit and cost of pollution can be balanced by maximizing (1.1) with respect to e. Setting to zero the derivative of (1.1) with respect to e yields the optimum amount of pollution:

$$e = M\delta/(\theta + \delta) \tag{1.2}$$

In this solution, the optimum e decreases with θ, because a large θ means the consumers dislike pollution intensely. The optimum increases with δ, because a large δ means pollution can help generate a large amount of output. Institutionally speaking, we can imagine the existence of a government that knows the parameters δ, θ and M of the production and utility functions, and finds the optimum amount of pollution (1.2) and controls pollution by setting actual amount of pollution equal to the optimum amount by regulation. Regulation may be achieved by prohibiting pollution in excess of the amount given by (1.2) or by requiring producers to use emission permits with a total amount given by (1.2).

The above formulation and solution of the problem of finding an optimum quantity of pollution are relevant for the measurement of "Green GDP". Green GDP is usually defined as GDP minus the damage of pollution to the environment when the output is produced. It presumably measures what GDP would be if we figure in the cost due to environmental deterioration in the course of producing the GDP. Let us assume that GDP has been produced with pollution e. As this section has emphasized, given the state of technology, in order to reduce pollution, GDP has to be reduced. Green GDP is the quantity of output which results after a designated amount of pollution is reduced. To compute Green GDP we need to know how much output will be sacrificed for a given reduction of pollution, or the price of reducing pollution. The pricing of pollution will be discussed at the end of Section 1.4. Green GDP will be further discussed at the end of Sections 4.2, 4.3, 4.5 and 4.6. A possible use of Green GDP is for the comparison of economic output in different years or among different regions. For such comparisons, Green GDP is more useful, because it nets out an important cost in producing the amount of output to be compared.

1.3.   Market Solution — The Invisible Hand

If the solution of Section 1.2 is achieved by some economic planner who is assumed to know the parameters δ, θ and M, what if the planner or the government does not have complete knowledge of these parameters? In this section, we show that if the consumers have the property right to the natural resource and can sell emission permits to the producers who have to acquire the permits for production, then the market solution is the optimum solution given by Equation (1.2).

We assume that consumers maximize utility subject to a budget constraint $c = qe$, where the value of consumption c (with price set equal to 1 per unit for normalization) equals income qe received by the consumers who sell e units of emission permits to the producers at price q per unit (relative to the price of consumer goods).

The consumers' problem is a problem of maximization subject to a constraint $c - qe = 0$ on the variables c and e. To solve this constrained maximization problem, we introduce a Lagrange multiplier λ and formulate a Lagrangean expression:

$$L = \log c + \theta \log(M - e) - \lambda(c - qe). \qquad (1.3)$$

To find a maximum we differentiate L with respect to the variables c and e to yield a set of first-order conditions:

$$c^{-1} = \lambda \quad \text{and} \quad \theta(M - e)^{-1} = q\lambda.$$

A supply equation of e is obtained by using c^{-1} in the first equation to substitute for λ in the second equation,

$$e = M - \theta c/q. \qquad (1.4)$$

Equation (1.4) shows that the higher the price q, the more emission permits the consumers will be willing to sell to the producers.

We assume the producers to maximize profit which equals the value of output minus its cost in paying for the pollution charge, or $Ae^{\delta} - qe$. Differentiating profit with respect to e and setting the result to zero, given output $y = Ae^{\delta}$, will yield a demand equation for e,

$$e = \delta y / q. \tag{1.5}$$

Equation (1.5) shows that the higher the price, the less will be the quantity demanded.

Under perfect competition, the profit of the producers is zero, implying that $y = qe = c$. Equating the supply of and the demand for e given by (1.4) and (1.5) gives the solution

$$e = M\delta / (\theta + \delta). \tag{1.6}$$

This is the same as the amount given in Equation (1.2) in Section 1.2, when the planner or the government is assumed to have complete knowledge of the parameter values to obtain the solution. The above is an example of the efficiency of a market solution when consumers and producers pursue their self-interests separately in the supply and demand for a commodity. An invisible hand ensures the optimum outcome.

If a market solution as presented above can guarantee the efficient allocation of natural capital, environmental problems must be due to a market failure. A market solution requires that the cost of damage to the environment be borne by the producer (in paying for the emission permits in the above discussion). In practice, however, the polluter often does not pay for the cost of pollution to society; he/she will overpollute and the natural resource is thereby overutilized. This case of market failure is generated by an "externality," which means an external effect of production (or consumption), the cost of which is not born by the producer (or consumer) who is responsible for this effect. An obvious solution to the problem of externalities, if it can be achieved, is therefore to design a scheme for the people responsible to pay for the cost of the external effects of their action (emissions). This section has provided an efficient market solution to the emission problem because the consumers can charge the full cost of emission to the producers, thus preventing the problem of externalities to occur.

In the model of this section, there is an important assumption required for the market solution to be optimum. It is the consumer's knowledge of the second term $\theta \log(M - e)$ of the utility function. In the case of air pollution, the consumer may know the discomfort of a certain amount of polluted air, but not its longer-term effect on his or her health. More to the point is the case of CO_2 emission. Consumers cannot feel the amount of CO_2 in the atmosphere, but even if they were to know the amount, they do not know the harm to society in years to come through the harmful effects on climate change. The parameters θ and M are uncertain. In Chapter 5, policy formulation under uncertainty will be discussed.

1.4. Implementation of a Government or a Market Solution to Pollution

Sometimes there are practical problems in giving the property rights of natural resources to the consumers and requiring them to collect fees from the producers. One solution to such problems is for the government to act on behalf of the consumers. To do so, the government itself will issue emission permits to the producers and use the revenue received to compensate the consumers. In addition, the consumers should be able to treat the government as an agent by forming an association that advises the government's environmental protection agency which decides the quantity of emission permits to issue. Given the quantity of permits, the price of each permit can be determined by the forces of demand and supply in the market as in the model of Section 1.3. I will return to this case in Chapter 4, when the use of a macroeconomic model to study pollution will be discussed. There may be institutional difficulties in putting the above-simulated market solution in practice, but the solution provides a conceptual framework that may be helpful in the design of solutions to environmental problems.

Once emission permits are sold by the government, incentives are provided for the producers to find cleaner production methods in order for them to reduce the cost of buying emission permits. The trading of emission permits issued to producers is also beneficial, because any free transaction benefits the parties involved. The producers having permits in excess can sell them to those in need. This rewards the producers using clean energy for production and punishes those who use a technology that pollutes more. The use of emission permits not only helps the efficient utilization of natural resources at present, but also encourages the adoption of clean technology for future production.

There are practical problems in the implementation of policies to control the amount of pollution, whether in the form of strict prohibition or paying for pollution permits. First is the need for monitoring, that is, to determine who is polluting and by how much. China has just begun to use satellites for monitoring some aspects of pollution. Second, there is a need to enforce the regulation, since producers may violate the law and actually pollute more than the amount permitted by law or regulation. Thirdly, there may be a need, as in the case of China, to impose a fine above the social cost of pollution. The reason is that potential pollution offenders figure on having some chance of not being caught and tend to make decision not according to the fine but to its expected value which is smaller. Fourthly, the cost of enforcement should be taken into account in the determination of the amount of emission allowed. If it is very costly to enforce, the benefit of setting a certain limit for pollution will be less than the case when there is no cost of enforcement. When the cost of enforcement is included, the benefit of having the same amount of clean air $(M - e)$ is reduced as it is more costly, i.e., θ in the utility function is reduced. According to equation (1.2), the optimum amount of pollution will be increased.

I can summarize the market solution of environmental problems as follows. Unlike other useful resources or assets, natural resources have been used freely without being paid for. This leads to abuse and waste. One way to protect the natural resources is to assign property rights of these resources to private citizens or to the government. A private owner will charge for the use of his resource by the largest amount that some users are willing to pay. Thus the resource will be used for the maximum benefit of the society. This illustrates the working of the "invisible hand" of Adam Smith to direct resources to be used for maximum benefit. If a resource is publicly owned, as land in China, the government official controlling it should apply the same principle. Like a private owner, he should not allow a piece of land to be developed today if he expects the land to yield more in the future. A corrupt government official tends to over-develop the land under his control while he is still in office. This is one reason for China's land to be over developed.

Therefore, a solution to the protection of the environment is to establish private ownership of natural resources. Property rights to the air or the water in a lake or river can be given to the citizens living in the neighborhood affected by pollution of the air or water. Under private ownership, the polluters have to pay the owners by purchasing from them permits for the amount of pollution (assuming it can be measured by some monitoring system). In the area affected, a specified number of pollution permits will be issued and distributed equally among the citizens. There will be demand for pollution permits by all industrial polluters and supply from all citizens. The market will determine the price of each permit. The total number of permits will be determined by the collective opinion of the citizens. After an initial number of permits are issued, if the citizens think that the air or water is too polluted, they can reduce the number of permits. Even if the number of emission permits issued is not optimal, the cost of any amount of pollution e can be measured by qe where q is the market price of each permission permit. This cost can be subtracted from the value of output to compute Green GDP.

1.5. Two Economies Sharing the Same Natural Resource

In the remainder of this chapter I will formulate several important models relevant to the study of environmental problems. The first is the case of two economies which share the same natural resource. This case is naturally treated as a two-person game.

Let player 1 solve his/her maximizing problem by using the following expression:

$$\log(Ae_1^{\delta 1}) + \theta_1 \log(M - e_1 - e_2).$$

Note that player 1 is assumed to know his own parameters $\delta 1$ and θ_1 in his utility function, and that the pollution e_2 by player 2 affects the utility of player 1. (This model can be easily general-ized by allowing M to be different for the two players.) Maximizing utility with respect to e_1 gives the following expression analogous to (1.2):

$$e_1 = (M - e_2)\delta 1/(\theta_1 + \delta 1) \qquad (1.7)$$

For player 2, we have a similar result:

$$e_2 = (M - e_1)\delta 2/(\theta_2 + \delta 2) \qquad (1.8)$$

In the (e_1, e_2) space, (1.7) and (1.8) are two linear reaction functions showing the optimal strategy e_1 of player 1 as a function of e_2, and the optimal strategy e_2 of player 2 as a function of e_1. A Nash equilibrium is given by the intersection of (1.7) and (1.8).

An interesting application of this example is to study the Nash equilibrium as a function of the four parameters $\delta 1$, $\delta 2$, θ_1 and θ_2 (and perhaps also of M_1 and M_2). In the dynamic game to be pre-sented in Section 1.7 as an extension of the model of this section, it would be interesting to explain the difference in attitude about global warming between rich and poor nations who have different parameter values. This dynamic game model may be used to explain the differ-ent attitudes of the poor and rich nations regarding the appropriate policy for controlling CO_2 emission. It may also be used to generate proposals to the United Nations or to members of an international conference on the optimal amounts of CO_2 emission for the rich and the poor countries as two players of this game.

1.6. Optimal Path for CO_2 Emission When the Problem is Multi-period

Let the utility function be a weighted sum of the one-period util-ity functions over time t. Let the total accumulation of CO_2 in the atmosphere at the beginning of year t be E_t and the amount of CO_2 emission in year t be e_t. Assume the dynamic relation:

$$E_{t+1} = b_1 E_t + b_2 e_t. \qquad (1.9)$$

Empirically $b_2 = 0.5$, that is, of the emission e_t of the current year only half will remain in the atmosphere at the beginning of the following year; $1 - b_1 = 1/400$ or $b_1 = 0.9975$, that is, of the accumulated emission E_t as of the beginning of year t, as much as 0.9975 will remain at the beginning of year $t + 1$.

In the language of optimal control or dynamic optimization, e_t is a control variable. It is a variable that, if the nations can agree, the world community can decide to achieve in each year t. E_t is a state variable. In the current optimal control problem, equation (1.9) is a dynamic equation that determines the state E_{t+1} at the beginning of the next period by the state E_t at the beginning of the current period and the control e_t in the current period.

An optimum control problem can be formulated either in discrete time or in continuous time. Our problem is formulated in discrete time. If formulated in continuous time, the objective function would be an integral rather than a sum, and the dynamic equation would be a differential equation for dE/dt. The problem can also be deterministic or stochastic. Our problem is a deterministic problem, since no random variables are involved. If a random residual is added to the right-hand-side of the above equation for E_t, the problem becomes stochastic. If the problem is formulated in continuous time, stochastic differential equations are used to describe the dynamics of the state variables.

This book does not require prior knowledge of optimal control. In a self-contained discussion, I will use a method for solving optimal control problems simply as an application of the method of Lagrange multipliers, first used in Chow (1970), later in Chow (1975) and in a more comprehensive way in Chow (1997). In Chapter 3, when I try to find an optimum path for CO_2 emission in the context of global warming I will explain the Lagrange method in detail.

Just to indicate how the Lagrange method can be applied in practice, consider the problem of this section, that is, to choose an optimal path for CO_2 emission e_t. For this problem we formulate the Lagrangean,

$$L = \Sigma_t \{ \beta^t [\log(A e_t^\delta) + \theta \log(M - E_t)] - \beta^{t+1} \lambda_{t+1} (E_{t+1} - 0.998 E_t - 0.5 e_t) \}. \tag{1.10}$$

In the expression (1.10) β is a discount factor, being slightly less than one to give less importance to utilities more distant in the future. Let there be only two periods with $t = 1$ and 2. The value of the state variable E_1 at the beginning of period 1 is taken as given. The only variables involved are e_1, e_2, E_2 and E_3 (the constraint on E_3 is required because E_2 and e_2 appear). Hence L can be considered as a function of these four variables. The first-order condition for its maximum can be obtained by taking the derivatives of (1.10) with respect to the four variables. In this function L for two periods we need two Lagrange multipliers λ_2 and λ_3, each for the constraint (1.9) for the corresponding period.

1.7. Optimal Paths of CO_2 Emission for Poor and Rich Economies

In order to understand why rich and poor countries disagree on the control of CO_2 emission, we can set up a dynamic game by using $\lambda_{t+1}(E_{t+1} - 0.998E_t - 0.5e_{1t} - 0.5e_{2t})$ for the dynamic constraint of each period and introducing different values of δ and θ for the two players (groups of economies). In this dynamic constraint, the emissions in the current year of both groups of economies will affect the total accumulated CO_2 in the atmosphere and thus the action of one group affects the action of the other group.

To obtain a Nash equilibrium of this dynamic game, each player i solves his dynamic optimization problem taking the other's solution e_j as given. Thus the optimal path e_{it} of player i is a function of the optimal path e_{jt} of the other player. Each player's problem is solved by setting up a Lagrangean involving his utility function and the above dynamic constraint and differentiating with respect to his control and state variables. A Nash equilibrium is reached when the reaction functions of both players yield the same pair of e_{1t} and e_{2t}. If player 1 represents the poor nations it may allow a higher level of emission than player 2.

We can also consider a Stackelberg solution with player 2 as the dominant player. The solution for player 1 is obtained first as a function of e_{2t}. Then the dominant player 2 considers this solution for player 1 as given and optimizes with respect to e_{2t}.

Table 1.1.   Tools to analyze four types of economic models.

	One economy	Several economies
Static — one period	Optimization	Game theory
Dynamic — many periods	Optimum control	Dynamic games

The analytical framework presented above can be summarized in Table 1.1.

This chapter has sketched the main ideas of environmental economics and the analytical methods that will be used to obtain an optimum amount or time paths of emission of pollutants. In Chapter 2, I will study China's environmental problems and policies. In the remaining chapters, besides applying the methods of this chapter to specific environmental problems, I will also discuss the problems of estimating macro-economic models taking into account pollution as a major variable, and of implementation of environmental policies.

After studying the optimal path for CO_2 emission in simple analytical models in Chapter 3 and the modeling of a macro-economy that incorporates pollution in Chapter 4, I will discuss the differences in policies for environmental protection between poor and rich regions or nations in Chapter 5.

Uncertainty is introduced in Chapter 6 that includes discussions of the question whether we need to be concerned with global warming now, of the modeling of the possible effect of expectations of the ill effects of global warming in the future on investment and thus on the evolution of the macro-economy, and of the effect of uncertainty on the optimum emission paths given in Chapter 4. Chapter 7 explains regional differences in environmental policies by applying game theory. Chapter 8 introduces two macro-economic models different from those in Chapter 4 to explain the phenomena of pollution and environmental protection. The second model of Chapter 8 adds scrubbing as an additional control variable. Chapter 9 deals with the use of emission permits, and Chapter 10 discusses the Environmental Kuznets curve.

Chapter 11 deals with clean energy and international efforts to solve environmental problems.

References

Andreoni, James and Arik Levison (2001). "The Simple Analytics of the Environmental Kuznets Curve." *Journal of Public Economics*, 89, 269–286.

Brock, W. A. (1973). "A polluted golden age," in: V. L. Smith, ed., *Economics of Natural and Environmental Resources*, New York: Gordon and Breach.

Chow, Gregory C. (1970). "Optimal Stochastic Control of Dynamic Economic Systems." *Journal of Money, Credit and Banking*, 2, 291–302.

Chow, Gregory C. (1975). *Analysis and Control of Dynamic Economic Systems*. New York: John Wiley and Sons.

Chow, Gregory C. (1997). *Dynamic Economics: Optimization by the Lagrange Method*. New York: Oxford University Press.

Maler, K. G. and J. R. Vincent, ed. 2005. *Handbook of Environmental Economics*, Elsevier.

Nordhaus, William D. and Joseph Boyer (2000). *Warming the World: Economic Models of Global Warming*. Cambridge, MA: MIT Press.

Smith, Adam. (2009). *The Wealth of Nations*. Management Laboratory Press.

Stern, Nicholas (2007). *The Economics of Climate Change: The Stern Review*. Cambridge and New York: Cambridge University Press.

Questions

1. Given the utility function:

$$\log c + \theta \log(M - p)$$

where c is consumption and p is pollution. Output y can be used for consumption or to clean up emission that requires k units of resource per unit of emission e. Let s be the amount of scrub or cleanup. The amount of output y used for cleaning up pollution is ks. Pollution $p = by - s$, where s is a constant.

a. Find the values s and y that maximize utility. As y increases, what will happen to the ratio of pollution to output y.

b. The environmental Kuznets Curve states that this curve is inverted U shape. Does your solution have this shape?

2. Provide a market solution to the problem of question 1.
3. Use Andreoni–Levison's utility or cost function as described in Chapter 10, derive an environmental Kuznets Curve.
4. Provide a market solution to question 3.

Chapter 2

China's Energy and Environmental Problems and Policies*

This chapter describes China's energy and environmental degradation problems in terms of air pollution, water pollution, CO_2 emission and shortage of energy. It discusses the laws enacted, agencies established and policies introduced to solve the energy–environment problems as well as the practical difficulties in the implementation of government environmental policies. Finally, it presents a proposal to improve the protection of China's natural environment.

2.1. Introduction

The economic activities of production and consumption require the use of energy, and the use of energy affects the environment in the forms of water pollution, air pollution and emission of CO_2 that causes global warming. Furthermore, the use of energy from exhaustible resources can create energy shortage in the future. The solutions to the problems of energy and environmental degradation include (1) reducing the use of energy in production and consumption, (2) increasing the use of energy-saving and environmentally friendly methods in production and consumption and (3) promoting technological innovations that will reduce the use of energy per unit of output (reduce energy intensity or increase energy efficiency) or reduce pollution per unit of output to achieve (1) and (2) in the

---

*This chapter is partly based on an article of the same title published in the *Asia-Pacific Journal of Accounting and Economics*, June 2008, and is updated thanks to helpful comments from Yuan Xu of the Chinese University of Hong Kong.

future. To achieve (1) and (2), given the state of technology, we can regulate the use of energy by law or by economic incentives to limit the emission of pollutants. The latter is an example in solving the problem of "externalities" in economics — the undesirable external effects of production or consumption, the cost of which is not born by the producer or consumer responsible. An economic solution to the problem of externalities is to charge the cost to the producer or consumer who is responsible.

In Section 2, we describe the energy–environment problems during China's recent economic development. In Section 3, we discuss the laws, government agencies established and the policies introduced by the Chinese government to protect the environment and reduce energy consumption. Section 4 deals with difficulties in implementing China's environmental policies. Section 5 discusses three most important issues related to the attempts to solve the energy–environment problem, and Section 6 concludes the chapter.

2.2. Environmental Problems in China

As pointed out in the Introduction, there are four aspects of the energy–environment problem, namely (1) air pollution, (2) water pollution, (3) the emission of CO_2 in the atmosphere that causes global warming, mainly from the burning of coal, and (4) shortage of future energy supply that relies on exhaustible resources.

2.2.1. Air Pollution

The air and water in China, especially in the urban areas, are among the most polluted in the world. According to a report of the World Health Organization (WHO) in 1998, of the ten most polluted cities in the world, seven can be found in China. Environmental pollution from coal combustion is damaging human health, air and water quality, agriculture and ultimately the economy. China is facing all four problems. Sulfur dioxide and soot caused by coal combustion are two major air pollutants, resulting in the formation of acid rain, which now falls on about 30% of China's total land area. Industrial boilers and furnaces consume almost half of China's coal and are the largest sources of urban air pollution. The burning of coal for cooking and heating in many cities accounts for the rest.

Another major source of air pollution is the use of oil and gasoline in the transportation sector, especially the emission from automobiles and jet engines. As the country becomes industrialized, pollution from both industrial and consumer sources will increase because of higher levels of output and consumption, the latter including the increase in the use of automobiles and in air travel, unless pollution per unit of output or consumption can be reduced.

2.2.2. *Water Pollution*

Mercury released into the air by coal-fired power plants is captured by raindrops and transferred to the soil, surface water and groundwater. Surface water affects the fish consumed. Groundwater is polluted by runoff from factories, smelters and mining operations, and then used by farmers downstream to irrigate their crops. Heavy use of fertilizers has contributed to contamination also. Fertilizers in China often contain high levels of metals, especially cadmium, which is harmful.

China's water is polluted also by the disposal of waste. There have been large quantities of deposits of organic and toxic waste from households, agriculture and industry. Deforestation has caused the flow of bud along the rivers and affects water supply and quality. *People's Daily* reports that Lake Taihu was covered with a foul-smelling algae and freshwater was shut off for more than 2 million people in Wuxi due to the blue-algae infestation of the lake. Besides the poor quality of water, there is the problem of the shortage of water. Water beds of several important cities, including Beijing and Shanghai, are low, causing shortage of supply of well water. Supply of water from rivers, including the Yellow River and the Yangtze River, is running short because of diversion to agriculture production and electricity generation along the sources.

2.2.3. *Energy Consumption*

According to *China Country Analysis Brief* published by the US Department of Energy (2001), China accounted for 9.8% of world energy consumption. By 2025, projections indicate that China will be responsible for approximately 14.2% of world energy consumption. Of the 40 quadrillion Btu of total primary energy consumed in China in 2001, 63% was coal, 26% was oil, 7% hydroelectricity and 3% natural gas. While residential consumption has increased its share of China's energy demand over the last decade, the largest increases in consumption were from the industrial sector. In 2001, China's energy intensity as measured by thousand Btu per 1990 dollars of output was as high as 36,000, as compared with 21,000 for Indonesia, 13,000 for South Korea, 4,000 for Japan and 11,000 for the United States, because of differences in output mix among these countries and in energy intensities in producing the same products.

While China ranks second in the world behind the United States in total energy consumption and carbon emissions, its per-capita energy consumption and carbon emissions are much lower than the world average. In 2001, the United States had a per-capita energy consumption of 341.8 million Btu, greater than 5.2 times the world's per-capita energy consumption and slightly over 11 times China's per-capita consumption. Per-capita carbon emissions are similar to energy consumption patterns. Compared to the world average of 1.1 metric tons, US emitted 5.5 metric tons of carbon per person, and China 0.6 metric tons of carbon per person. With a growing economy and increasing living standards, however, per-capita energy use and carbon emissions are expected to rise. Although per-capita energy use is relatively low, China's total consumption of energy and the resultant carbon emissions are substantial, due to the country's large population and heavy use of coal.

Concerning the possible shortage of future energy source, China imported 162.81 million tons of oil in 2006 as the world's second largest energy user. Its dependence on imported oil reached 47%, having increased by 4.1 percentage points from 2005. China's rapid increase in oil consumption will contribute to future shortage of this exhaustible resource.

2.2.4. CO_2 Emission

CO_2 emissions result in climate changes that affect the world's physical and biological systems. China's CO_2 emissions per person are now above the world's average. In 2013 China had 19% of the world's population but accounted for 27% of its CO_2 emissions. As of 2007 China has taken over the US, for the first time as the world's top producer of greenhouse gases. China is a non-Annex I country under the United Nations Framework Convention on Climate Change. This means that it has not agreed to binding emissions reductions in the Kyoto Protocol, which it rectified in August 2002. China's policies aim at cutting energy costs and reducing local pollution, rather than reducing carbon emissions for the benefit of the world.

People's Daily Online (June 4, 2007), reports the following facts:

According to the Initial National Communication on Climate Change of the People's Republic of China, the country's total greenhouse gas (GHG) emissions in 1994 are 4,060 million tons of carbon dioxide equivalent... Its total GHG emissions in 2004 is about 6,100 carbon dioxide equivalent, of which 5,050 million tons is carbon dioxide, 720 million is carbon dioxide equivalent of methane and 330 million is carbon dioxide equivalent of nitrous oxide. From 1994 to 2004, the average annual growth rate of GHG emissions is around 4 percent, and the share of carbon dioxide in total GHG emissions increased from 76 percent to 83 percent.

China's cumulative emissions of carbon dioxide from fossil fuel combustion accounted for only 9.33 percent of the world total during the period of 1959–2002, and the cumulative carbon dioxide emissions per capita are 61.7 tons over the same period, ranking the 92nd in the world.

Statistics from the International Energy Agency (IEA) indicate that per capita carbon dioxide emissions from fossil fuel combustion were 3.65 tons in 2004 in China, equivalent to only 87 percent of the world average and 33 percent of the level of the Organization for Economic Co-operation and development (OECD) countries.

Along with steady social and economic development, the emission intensity defined as the carbon dioxide emission per unit of GDP declined generally. According to the IEA, China's emission intensity fell to 2.76 kg carbon dioxide per U.S. dollar (at 1999 prices) in 2004, as compared to 5.47 kg carbon dioxide per U.S. dollar in 1990, a 49.5 percent decrease. For the same period, emission intensity of the world average dropped only 12.6 percent and of the OECD countries dropped 16.1 percent.

Since China is a developing country, it is not surprising that its per-capita CO_2 emission was only 87% of the world average and 33% of the level of the OECD countries. The concern is the rate of increase in China's per-capita CO_2 emission. There is a consensus in the scientific community that the level of total CO_2 in the atmosphere should not exceed a level equal to twice the level existing before the Industrial Revolution (see Pacala and Socolow, 2004). Exceeding that level could cause violently unstable weather, melting glaciers and prolonged draughts. If the rate of increase in emission in the future continues as it did in the last 30 years, this critical level could be reached in 50 years' time. Therefore, CO_2 emission is a critical and urgent problem. To obtain a global agreement on this issue is difficult, as shown by a week-long meeting of the Intergovernmental Panel on Climate Change in Bangkok, reported in an article in *San Francisco Chronicle* May 7, 2007.

For China to be willing to reduce its use of coal-fired power plants that cause CO_2 emission, alternative energy sources must be priced not higher than the price of power generated by coal. This will be possible if there shall be sufficient technological innovations in the production of clean energy at such low prices. Market incentives for such innovations have a good chance of success, according to Friedman (2007, p. 50).

Without the benefit of new technology, the world community can reduce the rate of increase of carbon emission by (1) using alternative energy to coal such as gas, nuclear, ethanol and solar, (2) reducing the consumption of electricity at homes, offices and factories, and (3) controlling the amount of CO_2 emission by reducing the burning of forests and capturing the amount of carbon from coal burning.

On (1), China is now the largest market for wind and solar energy. It has also increased the use of nuclear power although the effort was interrupted by the Fukushima accident.

2.3. Laws, Agencies and Policies for Protecting the Environment

2.3.1. Laws and Agencies for Environmental Protection

The Chinese Central Government has been aware of the environmental problems and has made serious attempts to protect and improve China's environment. In 1979, China passed the Environmental Protection Law for Trial Implementation. The 1982 Constitution included important environmental protection provisions. Article 26 of the Constitution requires that "the state protects and improves the environment in which people live and the ecological environment. It prevents and controls pollution and other public hazards." There are also provisions on the state's duty to conserve natural resources and wildlife. Based on these provisions a number of special laws have been enacted. These include the Water Pollution Prevention and Control Law of 1984, the Air Pollution Prevention and Control Law of 1987, the Water and Soil Conservation Law of 1991, the Solid Waste Law of 1995, the Energy Conservation Law of 1997 and several important international agreements, including the Kyoto and Montreal Protocols. Beginning in the late 1980s, Premier Li Peng, a nuclear engineer by training, issued statements underscoring the government's commitment to giving attention to environmental protection in its formulation and implementation of economic development policy. China's national legislature, through its promotion of "Cleaner Production" and other attempts to reduce air pollution, has significantly revised the Law on the Prevention and Control of Air Pollution in 2002.

New laws establishing comprehensive regulations have begun to curb the environmental damage. On the national level, policies are formulated by the State Environmental Protection Administration (SEPA) and approved by the State Council. The role of SEPA, which was established in 1998, is to disseminate national environmental policy and regulations, collect data and provide technological advice on both national and international environmental issues. In June 2002, China enacted the Cleaner Production Promotion Law, which established demonstration programs for pollution regulation in ten major Chinese cities, and designated several river valleys as priority areas. So far the laws are mainly of the regulation and control variety, rather than market-based policies such as taxing the polluters, partly because the government has not been able to design a set of appropriate market-based policies, e.g. to estimate the appropriate tax rate (more on this point in Section 3.3).

2.3.2. *Policies for Energy Saving*

On May 8, 2007, Premier Wen Jiabao made a speech stating that the current macrocontrol policy must focus on energy conservation and emission reduction in order to develop the economy while protecting the environment. The Chinese government had set a target of reducing energy consumption for every 10,000 yuan (1,298 US dollars) of GDP by 20% by 2010 (or 4% per year), while pollutant discharge (presumably measured by an index of quantities of different pollutants) should drop by 10%.

> To curb excessive growth of the sectors that consume too much energy and cause serious pollution, China must tighten land use and credit supply and set stricter market access and environmental standards for new projects amid efforts to rein in the rapid expansion of energy-gorging industries including power, steel, oil refinery, chemicals, construction materials, and metals.
>
> Restrictions should be imposed on exports in these sectors as soon as possible... We will continue to curb the energy-guzzlers by further adjusting exports rebates, levying more exports tariff, and reducing exports quotas... China will cancel preferential policies on the industries like lower tax, electricity and land costs.
>
> Outmoded production methods must be eliminated at a faster pace and how this policy is implemented by local governments and enterprises will be open to the public and subject to social supervision... The ten nationwide

energy saving programs, such as developing oil alternatives, upgrading coal-fired boilers and saving energy indoors, will save China 240 million tons of coal equivalent during the 2006–2010 period, including 50 million tons this year...

Note that Premier Wen's policy statements for environmental protection include (1) restricting the quantities of outputs, especially those that are environmentally polluting and high-energy consuming, by tightening land use and credit supply, (2) setting environmental standards for production, especially in new projects, and (3) improving method of production to make it environmentally friendly. Category (1) includes the restriction of exports which are produced by methods that are harmful to the environment by means of "adjusting exports rebates, levying more exports tariff, and reducing exports quotas".

2.3.3. Policies for Environment Protection by Regulation and Economic Incentives

China has set up a system for monitoring the discharge of pollutants but it is far from perfect because it relies on local government officials to implement the system. We will discuss the difficulties of implementing environmental policies in Section 4. For now we continue to examine the policies for environmental protection introduced, given the monitoring system, however imperfect.

To reduce the amount of sulfur dioxide emitted from the burning of coal in the factories, the Chinese government has imposed heavy penalties to such emissions and encouraged the building of equipment to capture sulfur dioxide. However, the use of such equipment is costly even after it is built, and many factories do not use it except when they are being inspected. More recently the government is trying to introduce the use of monitoring device to measure the amount of sulfur dioxide emission coming out of each plant, but such a monitoring system has not yet been put into practice effectively.

China is also using economic incentives to solve the problem of externalities resulting from the use of energy. To reduce the use of coal and encourage a switch to cleaner burning fuels, the government has introduced a tax on high-sulfur coals. A system of emissions trading for sulfur dioxide, similar to that used in the United States, is being tested in some cities with pilot projects and may eventually be applied nationwide. The Chinese government will advance reforms in the pricing of natural gas, water and other resources, raise the tax levied on pollutant discharge, establish a "polluter pays" system and severely punish those who violate the environmental protection laws. To ensure that fees charged on pollutants are higher than abatement costs and to strengthen existing laws, the government is considering the imposition of large fines on pollutant emissions. The rationale for charging higher fees than the abatement cost may be the expected imperfect enforcement. Potential polluters will equate expected fine (equal to the fee charged times the probability of getting caught) to the benefit of abatement. Future Chinese environmental initiatives also may include formulating a tax structure beneficial to environmental protection and granting preferential loans and subsidies to enterprises that construct and operate pollution treatment facilities. The government will also provide incentives to companies that use more energy-efficient production facilities and techniques.

Besides economic incentives, efforts are made to introduce technologies that will treat wastewater, prevent air pollution and improve environmental monitoring systems. Because of the above-mentioned government policies, state and non-state enterprises have tried to find cleaner technology to generate power than from coal. Governments of cities such as Shanghai have tried to adopt urban planning strategies that are environment friendly. Space within a city is reserved for planting trees in order to improve air quality. Travelers to Beijing, Shanghai and Guangzhou in years 1998 to 2000 could witness that these cities became cleaner and the air quality was improved during this period.

2.3.4. Policies on CO_2 Emission

Policies for reducing the emission of CO_2 *per se* are still under negotiation among nations. China appears to be more concerned with the problems of air and water pollution since the CO_2 emission problem is less urgent for China. A recent expression of China's policy of limited involvement in the prevention of global warming is a statement of President Hu Jintao on June 7, 2007, during the G8 meetings in Germany that calls for upholding the principle of "common but differentiated responsibilities" for developing countries in tackling climate change. "We should work together to make sure the international community upholds the goals and framework established in the United Nations Framework Convention on Climate Change and its Kyoto Protocol (in 1997) and the principle of common but differentiated responsibilities" while he said that developing countries should also carry out "active, practical and effective cooperation..."

He stated that

> Considering both historical responsibility and current capability, developed countries should take the lead in reducing carbon emission and help developing countries ease and adapt to climate change... For developing countries, achieving economic growth and improving the lives of our people are top priorities. At the same time, we also need to make every effort to pursue sustainable development in accordance with our national conditions.

Climate change, which could cause swelling sea levels and climate swings, was a major issue at the G8 summit from June 6 to June 8, 2007. Kyoto Protocol, which requires industrialized countries to cut greenhouse gas emission by 5% from 1990 levels was to expire in 2012. Parties concerned hope to launch negotiations for its replacement at an early date. Skepticism, however, was evident at the summit for reaching a fixed, quantifiable targets for reducing the greenhouse gas emission. (See *People's Daily Online*, June 8, 2007.)

In the mean time, a multinational effort needs to be made to limit the emission of CO_2. As pointed out previously, if the level of carbon dioxide reaches twice the level existing before the Industrial Revolution great climate instability will occur. How to achieve an international political consensus to reduce the rate of increase with each country taking its fair share so as not to exceed the above critical level is a most pressing problem today. A solution to this problem is proposed in Section 9.5. Note that China has some incentives to reduce emissions as it receives benefits from the Clean Development Mechanism (CDM), an arrangement under the Kyoto Protocol that allows industrialized countries with a greehouse gas reduction commitment (called Annex 1 countries) to invest in projects that reduce emissions in developing countries as an alternative to more expensive emission reductions in their own countries.

2.3.5. *Development of Clean and Renewable Energy*

China regards the creation of clean and renewable energy as an important national policy and is developing hydropower, solar power, wind power, natural gas, biomass fuel and methane under its 11th Five-Year Plan. Current efforts to offset coal consumption include the development of natural gas and coal-bed methane infrastructure, increasing the number of combined heat and power plants, adding approximately 3,000 megawatts (MW) of hydropower annually, and developing renewable energy resources such as wind and photovoltaics for electricity generation.

For China's electricity generation, renewable sources of energy (including hydroelectricity) accounted for 18.6% in 2001, second to coal. With assistance from the United Nations and the United States, China hopes to embark on a multi-milliondollar renewable energy strategy to combat pollution. Wind resources are concentrated in the northern and western regions of China, as well as along the coast, and are suitable for both rural village electrification and large-scale, grid-connected electricity production. The highest wind potential in China lies along the coast and the offshore islands, in or near many of the major population centers. The next highest wind potential region covers Inner Mongolia and the northern Gansu Province, both of which are home to numerous villages with no access at present to grid-based electricity.

Current utilization of solar energy includes small-scale uses, such as household consumption, television relays and communications, but it is increasing steadily, especially in the number of solar kitchen ranges to substitute for the use of coal.

While solar and wind power provide significant renewable energy potential, China's growth in renewable energy in the 2010s will be dominated by hydropower, particularly with completion of the 18.2-GW Three Gorges Dam project in 2009. Although the Three Gorges Dam is seen as both an important source of energy for China's growing electricity consumption needs and a means of taming the Yangtze River, notorious for its disastrous floods, the controversial dam also could prove to be an environmental disaster. So far, few attempts have been made to address concerns regarding the accumulation of toxic materials and other pollutants from industrial sites that will be inundated after construction of the dam. Other social costs of the dam and the use of hydropower in general include displacement of people and impact on fisheries.

By 2025, the share of nuclear power used for China's electricity generation is expected to increase to 4% from the little over than 1% at present. The use of nuclear power can be considered a very promising alternative energy source if the problem of disposing its waste can be properly handled. (See Appendix: At present, China's mainland has 11 nuclear reactors at six plants, all on the east coast, with a combined installed capacity of 9.07 million kW. Of the 11 reactors, three use domestic technologies, two are equipped with Russian technology and four with French technologies, and two are Canadian designed. All the 11 reactors employ second-generation nuclear power technologies. To meet its economic growth, the country planned to have 40 million kW of installed nuclear capacity on its mainland by 2020, which would be 4% of the projected electricity supply capacity, or double the current level.)

2.4. Problems of Policy Implementation and Law Enforcement

As an example of failure to implement government environmental policies, consider the statement of Premier Wen Jiabao in April 2007 as reported in Section 2.3.2. The quoted speech of Premier Wen states:

> The challenge of reducing energy consumption and greenhouse gas emissions has proved arduous as China's economy grew 11.1% in the first quarter (of 2007) but power consumption surged 14.9%... Energy consumption as a

fraction of GDP fell only 1.23% in 2006, well short of the annual goal of 4% (as stated in the 11th Five-Year Plan of 2006–2010).

The positive aspect of the above story is that, unlike other developing countries such as India, South Korea and Brazil, China was able to reduce both the amount of energy and carbon consumed per dollar of GDP somewhat over the past two decades. The reduction of energy intensity was made possible by its very high level to begin with, the efforts by the Chinese government to conserve energy, and the adoption of more modern industrial plant and equipment. China's Energy Conservation Law came into effect on January 1, 1998. Further efforts by the government to increase overall energy efficiency have included the reduction of coal and petroleum subsidies. Coal consumption is again rising, however, after declining in the late 1990s, and China's energy intensity increased slightly in 2001. At the same time, the government has promoted a shift toward lesser energy-intensive services and higher value-added products as well as encouraged the import of energy-intensive products.

The failures in meeting policy targets such as reducing energy intensity by 4% per year are the results partly of the unrealistic nature of the targets and partly of the failure to implement laws and policies by the Chinese government in general, including those to protect the environment. Besides the reduction of the use of energy per unit of output, a more important way to protect the environment is to control the emission of pollutants in production that uses the same amount of energy or to use clean energy. Laws to control such emissions are not effectively enforced. Chinese producers violate environmental protection laws to reduce cost of production. More importantly, local government officials do not cooperate in enforcing such laws. It is often to the advantage of local governments to allow pollution to take place illegally in order to promote a higher rate of economic growth, and the central government has not been able to control them. Local government officials benefit from higher levels of output in their region as they receive credits for economic development and sometimes bribes from polluting producers. These factors will continue to hinder the enforcement of environmental laws for some time to come.

However, there are also factors contributing to successful implementation of laws and policies to protect the environment. One is the strong resolve of the central government. The National People's Congress enacted on October 28, 2007, a Law on Conserving Energy by stating that work carried out by local government officials in energy conservation should be integrated into the assessment of their political performance along side with output growth. The second is that, if it wishes, the central or local government has the power to enforce such laws because the operation of an industrial enterprise requires its approval and sometimes even its assistance in the provision of land or credit. In order to protect and improve the environment the government not only can punish the offender but also provide economic incentives for people to act for the economic welfare of the society. There are a number of incentive schemes adopted by the Chinese government for industrial producers as we have described in Section 2.3.3. Wheeler, Dasgupta and Wang (2003) provided econometric evidence to show that pollution levy does have a negative effect on the quantity of water and air pollution per unit of output. Third, there is a positive income effect on the demand for a clean environment. As the Chinese economy gets more developed, the demand for cleaner water and air will increase, and the Chinese people can afford to pay for it. In the long run, though not necessarily in the near future, this favorable income effect should more than offset the unfavorable effect of producing a large quantity of output as the experience of the developed economies has demonstrated.

Since the control of pollution resulting from production using existing technology is difficult, one way for environment protection is to promote the use of clean energy by reducing its price relative to the price of existing energy. This can be achieved by imposing a cost to using polluting energy (which is hard to enforce) or by promoting technological innovations for the development of clean energy, especially to replace the use of coal. There are incentives in the free market for such innovations to take place. In addition, the government can promote such innovations by subsidy and tax policies if it can identify them correctly.

Economy and Lieberthal (2007) appealed to multinationals doing business in China to play a positive role in protecting China's environment by setting an example for practicing environment-friendly production while impressing the Chinese government of such conduct in their pursuit of profits. If it is to the self-interest of the multinationals to do so, one wonders why this would not be to the self-interest of domestic Chinese firms also. If such an undertaking is to their self-interest why have the multinationals and Chinese domestic enterprises failed to pursue it? Why are the multinationals and the Chinese enterprises so ignorant of their self-interests in this regard?

Rather than relying on multinational institutions to assist in environmental protection, the Chinese central government needs to enforce the laws for protecting the environment more strictly. A major hindrance to environmental law enforcement is the lack of cooperation on the part of local government officials who are interested in increasing output of their own regions. The central government needs to establish and monitor a clear set of environmental standards and severely punish the governor of the violating province even by relieving him of his position. When Zhu Rongji was President of the People's Bank in the 1990s, he succeeded in restricting the quantity of money supply by enforcing the policy that the President of a provincial People's Bank would be replaced if the extension of credit in his province were to exceed the quota set by the Central Bank. The same method for the enforcement of environmental policy may be needed. Given the risk of such a severe punishment a provincial governor would apply the same policy to enforce environmental standards in cities and counties in his province by similarly punishing the mayors and county officials. It is hoped that the central government will have a strong resolve to enforce environmental policies as suggested above.

2.5.   A Proposal to Improve the Protection of China's Natural Environment

There are two major aspects of the problem of environment protection. The first is to decide what to regulate and how to regulate. For example, in the case of pollution, the government has to decide how much pollution should be allowed in each situation and whether the method should be a regulation to limit pollution or the issuance of emission permits which can be traded in the market. The second is to enforce the laws for environmental protection effectively. In China, laws regulating pollution have often been violated.

The proposal presented here is aimed at solving both aspects of the problem. One basic proposition in economics is that resources will be efficiently allocated in the market when sellers controlling a resource try to get the most in selling it to buyers who also try to economize in its use. In such a situation, there will be no waste. In the case of a natural resource like air and water in the environment, there are no private owners controlling it, and users do not pay for using it, thus creating waste in the use of this resource. For a discussion of environmental economics the reader may refer to Uzawa (2005) and Tietenberg (2007). Imagine the possibility of giving property rights of the atmosphere to consumers who can sell it to producers in the form of emission permits at market price. The market forces of demand for and supply of emission permits would make the amount of air pollution optimal — not too much to ruin the environment excessively but enough to allow enough production to take place.

To improve the regulation of China's industrial air and water pollution, I propose the use of emission permits in the following way.

First, all citizens of an affected region (which is large enough to take the effect of pollution from neighboring regions as given) are assumed to have the right of the air (or water) in his region. Through their representatives (the village heads elected by popular votes in rural areas and district representatives publicly elected in urban areas) the total amount of pollution allowed in the region is decided, possibly by a median of the votes cast by the representatives. Second, given the total number of permits in the region, each citizen is entitled to the same number of emission permits and can sell his share to the potential polluters. The permission permits can be traded also among the polluters. Note that in this proposal, no industrial polluter will be given permits for free. The reason is that the act of pollution uses up natural resources and the user should pay for the cost of it, however small the amount. Given the number of permits issued, demand by potential polluters will determine the price per permit.

In applying this proposal to regulate industrial water and air pollution in China, we have to accept the fact that the regional office of the Ministry of Environment Protection has the right to issue emission permits. Our proposal suggests that the regional office accept, or at least seriously consider, the recommendation of the representatives of the citizens in determining the total number to be issued. The proceeds from the permits sold to the polluters should be returned to the citizens equally. This can be done by distributing the receipts to the regional government for the representatives to decide how they should be used for the citizens, including giving them an equal share of the receipts.

In short the proposal consists of the following four components:

(1) For each case of air or water pollution the regional office of the Ministry of Environmental Protection issues a fixed number of emission permits per quarter. Each polluter is required to report the amount of pollution during the quarter and to pay for a number of permits equal to the amount of pollution reported.

(2) Given the number of permits issued, demand by polluters will determine the price per permit. The Administration's local office will first set an initial price for the permits. If the price is too low, the permits will run out and some polluters need to purchase them from others. If the initial price is too high, there will be unsold permits and the local office will lower the price until all permits are sold.

(3) In determining the number of permits to issue in each region affected by the pollution, the local office solicits and respects suggestions from the directly elected village heads in rural areas and the directly elected representatives in urban areas.

(4) The revenue received from the permits will be returned to the local government of the area affected, to be used for the benefit of the citizens as determined by their representatives including paying them an equal share of the revenue received. Under the proposal the local residents, through their representatives and the local government, will have an incentive not only to determine a suitable amount of pollution permitted but also to help enforce the amount.

This proposal echoes two major directions of China's development: (1) market reform and (2) promotion of a democratic government. Under the proposal, market-oriented policies to regulate air and water pollution would be formulated democratically. The people would help to not only formulate such policies but also enforce them.

To economize the cost of monitoring, the amount of emission in each industrial establishment needs to be determined. Each establishment is required to submit the amount of its pollution on which the number of required permits is based. False amount submitted, if discovered, will lead to severe punishment. The citizens can be encouraged to report on larger amounts than submitted when they observe such instances.

The above hypothetical market solution to the problem of air or water pollution is not directly feasible for China or for any country. However, the basic underlying principle can be employed as a means of introducing practical institutional arrangements for the Chinese government, or another government, to protect the environment. The requirement of the institutional arrangements is that the government issues air or water pollution permits to producers or users of such natural resource on behalf of the consumers or as an agent of the consumers. For example, an association representing the consumers in each locality in China can be given authority to decide how many permission permits the local government in the area should issue. Given the total number of emission permits as approved by the consumer association, the permits can be traded at prices determined by the market. The revenue received will be distributed to the consumers through the above association. Hence both the supply of emission permits by the consumers, acting through the government, and the demand for emission permits (or for the use of the natural resource concerned) will be based on economic calculations to arrive at an optimum quantity and a suitable price in the use of natural resource provided in the environment.

The proposed solution will also help in solving the second aspect of the problem of environmental protection. The consumers will try to deter violators in order to protect their revenue from pollution.

Both industrial polluters and local government officials who are more concerned with rapid growth in output in their locality than with protecting the environment have contributed to the violation of environmental protection laws in China. Chinese citizens, in cooperation with officials representing the central government to protect the environment, would help to enforce environmental protection laws and regulations in ways which they deem appropriate and which are allowed under the institutional arrangement to be established to put this proposal into practice. The violation of environmental protection laws has resulted in damage to the environment and protests of Chinese citizens. This proposal attempts to channel the energy of the protesting citizens to positive action through government channels.

In its present form, the above proposal is only conceptual. Much remains to be done in utilizing the concepts advanced above to design precise institutional arrangements for Chinese citizens to participate in the protection of the natural environment for their interest and for the interest of the country. Two points should be noted here. First, I do not mean that this proposal is applicable to all cases of environmental protection in China. There are cases when direct regulation on the amount of emission allowed may be appropriate. Second, in terms of implementation, the mechanism used to collect profit tax from enterprises can be used to collect fees for pollution also. Of course, monitoring the amount of pollution is required for the protection of the environment in any case.

2.6. Conclusions

Let me state the following six important points to conclude this chapter.

1. China's environmental problems are serious, and the government has been aware of it since the early 1990s and has tried hard to solve them.
2. Enforcement of environmental protection laws is difficult because local government officials often do not cooperate.
3. I propose, first, a stricter enforcement of environmental protection laws by removing negligent provincial governors from office, and,

second, by giving the consumers the power and opportunity to regulate the amount of pollution by the use of emission permits in cooperation with government officials.

4. In spite of all efforts, the Chinese people will suffer the consequences of environmental degradation for some time to come.
5. Looking further into the future, one can be optimistic because there is a positive income effect on the demand for a clean environment and there will be important technological innovations to discover alternative clean energy.
6. In the near future, the environmental problem is not serious enough to hamper the rapid growth of China's economy, which is driven by the fundamental forces of high-quality human capital, a working set of market institutions and a gap from the most advanced technology which enables China to grow fast to catch up as discussed in Chow (2015).

References

Chow, Gregory C. (2015). *China's Economic Transformation.* 3rd edn., Chapter 10. UK: Wiley. Forthcoming.

Department of Energy, US Government, "China Country Analysis Brief." http://www.eia.doe.gov/emeu/cabs/chinaenv.html

Economy, Elizabeth and Kenneth Lieberthal (2007). "Scorched Earth: Will Environmental Risks in China Overwhelm its Opportunities?" *Harvard Business Review*, June, pp. 88–96.

Friedman, Thomas L. (2007). "The Power of Green: What does America Need to Regain its Global Stature." *The New York Times Magazine*, April 15, Section 6, pp. 40–67.

Pacala, Stephen and Robert Socolow (2004). "Stabilization Wedges: Solving the Climate Problem for the Next 50 Years with Current Technologies." *Science*, Vol. 305, Issue 5686, August 13, 968–972.

Tietenberg, Tom (2007). *Environmental Economics and Policy.* New York: Pearson Addison Wesley.

Uzawa, Hirofumi (2005). *Economic Analysis of Social Common Capital.* Cambridge: Cambridge University Press.

Wheeler, David, Susmita Dasgupta and Hua Wang (2003). "Can China Grow and Safeguard its Environment? The Case of Industrial

Pollution." Chapter 12 of Hope, Nicholas, Dennis Tao Yang and Mu Yang Li, ed. *How Far Across the River? Chinese Policy Reform at the Millennium.* Stanford: Stanford University Press, http://www. stanford.edu/group/siepr/cgi-bim/siepr/?q=system/files/shared/ pubs/papers/pdf/credpr68.pdf

Appendix

China to Build Five Nuclear Power Stations in 2009

People's Daily, April 20, 2009

China plans to build five nuclear power stations in the eastern and southern regions this year, the country's energy planner said here on Monday.

The five projects will be constructed in the coastal Zhejiang Province, Shandong Province and southern Guangdong and Hainan provinces, the National Energy Administration (NEA) announced at a meeting on nuclear power application.

The construction of the Sanmen Nuclear Power Plant in Zhejiang has already begun Sunday.

It would be the first third-generation pressurized water reactor in the country using AP 1000 technologies developed by US-based Westinghouse, and also the first in the world using such technologies.

The first generating unit with a capacity of 1.25 million kw was expected to start operation in 2013. The plant will eventually have six such units.

"We will build more generating units with AP 1000 technologies and introduce them to inland provinces based on the construction and operation of the Sanmen project," said Sun Qin, vice head of NEA.

The first three inland nuclear power plants in Hubei, Hunan and Jiangxi provinces were likely to get approval for construction by the end of this year or early next year, the administration said.

Of the five projects scheduled for 2009, the Shandong Rongcheng Nuclear Power Plant, will begin its construction phase in September.

The project, with a generating capacity of 200,000 kw, will be domestically-designed and equipped with some fourth-generation nuclear reactor technologies, according to the NEA.

Details of the other three projects were not provided at the meeting.

At present, China's mainland has 11 nuclear reactors at six plants, all on the east coast, with a combined installed capacity of 9.07 million kw.

Of the 11 reactors, three use domestic technologies, two are equipped with Russian technology and four with French technologies, and two are Canadian designed. All the 11 reactors employ second-generation nuclear power technologies.

To meet its economic growth, the country planned to have 40 million kw of installed nuclear capacity on its mainland by 2020, which would be 4 percent of projected electricity supply capacity, or double the current level.

Source: Xinhua

Chapter 3

Optimal Path for CO$_2$ Emission to Control Global Warming

3.1. Introduction

Global warming due to the emission of CO$_2$ has attracted a lot of attention in recent years. Al Gore received a Nobel Peace Prize in 2007 because of his effort to call the world's attention to this problem. On December 7, 2009, the UN Climate Change Conference opened in Copenhagen, with most of the countries in the world. On 18 December 2009, after about two weeks of consultations and negotiations, delegates finally agreed on the so-called Copenhagen Accord. However, the Copenhagen Accord is not legally binding and does not commit countries to agree to a binding successor to the Kyoto Protocol, which ends in 2012.

On the topic of climate change, many experts claim that the total amount of CO$_2$ in the atmosphere E should not exceed a critical level of 600 GtC (gigatons of carbon equivalent) above which violent climate changes would occur, while its current level is 200 GtC. The current amount of annual emission is $e = 8$ GtC/yr. According to a *New York Times* editorial (p. A22, August 18, 2009) atmospheric concentration of greenhouse gases, now about 380 parts per million, should not be allowed to exceed 450 parts per million, but keeping accumulated emissions below that threshold would require stabilizing them by 2015 or 2020, and actually reducing them by at least 60% by 2050. To keep the steady state level of E at 600, we need to reduce e from 8 to 3. The number 3 is derived from the dynamic relation

$$E_{t+1} = b_1 E_t + b_2 e_t, \qquad (3.1)$$

where E_t denotes the cumulated amount of CO$_2$ at the beginning of year t and e_t denotes the amount of emission during year t. Empirically $b_2 = 0.5, 1 - b_1 = b_2/200$ and $b_1 = 0.9975$ (see, e.g.,

Socolow and Lam 2006). (The denominator 200 actually increases with time, roughly by 1% every year.)

Equation (3.1) means that half of the emission in the current year will remain in the atmosphere at the beginning of the next year. Of the total accumulation in the atmosphere at the beginning of this year, $1 - (0.5/200)$, or 99.75%, will remain at the beginning of the next year. At the steady state, when $E_{t+1} = E_t = E$ and $e_t = e$, solving the above equation gives $E = 200\,e$. If $E = 600$, e has to be 3, much lower than the current level 8.

One important question in the study of global warming to be addressed in this chapter is how to reduce annual CO_2 emission from $8\,GtC/yr$ to $3\,GtC/yr$. Should e first increase from 8 and then decline later to reach 3, or should it start decreasing immediately and gradually from 8 to 3? What is the most desirable time path of e_t from here onward? Many scholars have provided answers to this question. The economic approach suggested in this chapter is to evaluate the cost of having amount E of accumulated CO_2 in the atmosphere and the benefit that emission e will bring to increase production at each period; the discounted values of the costs and benefits for all future years will be summed up in order to judge whether one path for e to go from 8 to 3 is better than another path. Since the costs and benefits of all future years can be summarized by a multi-period objective function, we need to solve an optimal control problem to determine the optimum path of future CO_2 emission e to maximize the value of the objective function.

In this chapter, I consider the derivation of optimal paths for the amount e of CO_2 emission in the context of the simple objective function of Chapter 1.[1] In this discussion, I abstract from the problems of having capital and labor in production, of capital accumulation and of estimation of economic models incorporating these features. These problems will be discussed in the context of a macroeconomic model of one country in Chapter 4. After setting up a simple model of dynamic optimization (or optimal control, as the two terms can

---

[1]For a helpful reference, see also Kolstad and Toman's (2005) survey paper which addresses climate policy and the optimal paths of CO_2 emission as well.

be used interchangeably), I will present in Section 3.2 the Lagrange method for solving dynamic optimization problems that will be used in many applications of this book, including a numerical method for solving optimal control problems. Section 3.3 deals with the optimum time path e_t of CO_2 emission for a model that does not take into account possible inertia of changing the value of e from year to year or of changing the growth rate in e from $\Delta e(t-1)$ to $\Delta e(t)$ while the model in Section 3.4 does. Section 3.5 presents numerical results of a selected dynamic optimization model to solve for the optimum path of CO_2 emission. Section 3.6 discusses a model of Socolow and Lam (2006) which solves the same problem using a different framework that does not consider the tradeoff between the cost in utility and the benefit in production of CO_2 emission. It will be interesting to compare the optimal path of their solution with ours.

In much of the discussion in this chapter and in the technical parts of this book, specific utility functions are employed, and derivation of optimum control results is worked through using the specific utility functions. There is much to be learned in working through examples for particular parametric utility functions. First, the use of parametric analysis in a specific model helps one think quantitatively about environmental problems. Second, it facilitates statistical estimation of the parameters. Third, understanding of the general case often follows from first working out the solution of specific cases. Mathematicians who prove general theorems often start working with specific examples that provide them with intuition and insights for the general case. They later summarize the results as a general theorem. Finally this book is devoted to solving particular problems rather than proving general mathematical propositions. We introduce particular mathematical models and methods in order to analyze environmental problems.

3.2. An Exposition of the Lagrange Method for Solving Optimal Control Problems

The Lagrange method will be explained in this section and motivated by the problem of finding an optimum path for CO_2 emission stated in Section 3.1. In this problem we assume the same utility function as given in Chapter 1 and the dynamic Equation (3.1) for the total accumulation E_{t+1} of CO_2 in the atmosphere at the beginning of period t, which depends on past accumulation and the emission $e(t)$ of the current period.

The utility function we have chosen is

$$\log(Ae_t^\delta(M - E_t)^\theta) = \log A + \delta \log(e_t) + \theta \log(M - E_t).$$

Ae_t^δ is output produced by a production function with capital and labor taken as given. The variable $(M - E_t)$ allows E to have a negative effect on utility and the effect is detrimental when E is close to M; its logarithm approaches minus infinity as E approaches M. The parameter θ measures the relative importance of having more current emission e_t for the increase in output and the damage caused by having a larger quantity E_t of accumulated CO_2 in the atmosphere. We rescale this utility function by dividing it by δ or by setting $\delta = 1$. The redefined utility function $Ae_t(M - E_t)^\theta$ can be interpreted as an index of world output net of the harmful effect of the amount E of accumulated CO_2 in the atmosphere. In the literature on global warming there are estimates of the percentage change of world output resulting from an increase in mean temperature caused by a change in $M - E$ by one percentage point, namely estimates of the parameter θ. An estimate of θ will be used to calculate the optimum path of e_t numerically.

Given the utility function $\log(Ae_t(M - E_t)^\theta)$ and the dynamic Equation (3.1) which determines the state variable E_{t+1} as a function of E_t and the control variable e_t we can set up a dynamic optimization problem to determine the optimum time path for the emission e_t.

Since for each period t we maximize a given utility function subject to a dynamic constraint, when we maximize a weighted sum (weighted by the discount factor β^t) of the utility functions each subject to the constraint for that period we can apply the Lagrange method using a Lagrangean expression of the form

$$L = \Sigma\{\beta^t[\log(e_t) + \theta \log(M - E_t)]$$
$$- \beta^{t+1}\lambda_{t+1}[E_{t+1} - b_1 E_t - b_2 e_t]\}. \tag{3.2}$$

A set of first-order conditions for an optimum can be obtained by differentiating (3.2) with respect to the control and state variables for each period. The resulting equations are functional equations for the control variable e_t and the Lagrange multipliers λ_t as functions of the state variable E_t. In general, these functional equations do not have analytical solutions.

A numerical solution to an optimum control problem formulated as the maximization of a Lagrangean such as expression (3.2) can be obtained by approximating the dynamic equation for its state variable by a linear function and its objective function by a quadratic function. To pursue this approach we formulate a "linear-quadratic" optimum control problem using the Lagrangean

$$L = \Sigma_{t=1}^{T}\{\beta^t(x_t - a_t)'R_t(x_t - a_t)\}/2$$
$$- \beta^t\lambda_t'[x_t - b - Ax_{t-1} - Cu_{t-1}]\}. \tag{3.3}$$

Treating a more general case we let x_t be a column vector of p state variables, u_t be a column vector of q control variables, a_t be a vector of specified targets for x_t to approach, R_t be a given symmetric matrix in the utility function, a_t be a vector of targets for the state variables x_t and λ_t' be a row vector of Lagrange multipliers for period t, with prime denoting transpose. In the dynamic equation for x_t, b is a given column vector of p components, A is a given $p \times p$ matrix and C is a given $p \times q$ matrix. Since we are dealing with a vector of p state variables, we need a vector of p Lagrange multipliers for each period. Our objective is to maximize L by choosing the optimum policies u_0 to u_{T-1}.

We will find the optimum for the control variable u_t period by period backward in time beginning with period T. Given the optimum u_{T-1}, we find the optimum u_{T-2} that maximizes the objective function for the last two periods. Given the optimum u_{T-1} and u_{T-2}, we find the optimum u_{T-3} that maximizes the objective function for the last three periods and so forth. In this way, maximizing a function of T variables, $u, u_1, \ldots, u_{T-1}$ is reduced to maximizing T functions of one variable each, which is much easier than the first problem. This procedure is valid when the objective function is a sum of utility functions each for one period. The technical material below can be skipped if the reader is interested only in the results.

For period T we maximize

$$L_T = \beta^T (x_T - a_T)' R_T (x_T - a_T)/2$$
$$- \beta^T \lambda'_T [x_T - b - Ax_{T-1} - Cu_{T-1}]. \tag{3.4}$$

Using the differentiation rules for a vector z and a symmetric matrix A

$$\partial(u'z)/\partial u = \partial(z'u)/\partial u = z \quad \text{and} \quad \partial(u'Au)/\partial u = 2Au,$$

we set to zero the partial derivatives of β^{-T} times L_T with respect to the (vector) control variable u_{T-1} and the (vector) state variable x_T to obtain

$$C'\lambda_T = 0, \tag{3.5}$$

$$R_T(x_T - a_T\} - \lambda_T = 0. \tag{3.6}$$

Premultiplying (3.6) by C' and using (3.5) we have

$$C'R_T(b + Ax_{T-1} + Cu_{T-1} - a_T\} = 0. \tag{3.7}$$

The solution for the optimum u_{T-1} as a function of the state x_{T-1} is

$$u_{T-1} = -(C'R_TC)^{-1}C'R_T(Ax_{T-1} + b - a_T)$$
$$= G_T x_{T-1} + g_T \tag{3.8}$$

where we have defined

$$G_T = -(C'R_TC)^{-1}C'R_TA, \tag{3.9}$$

$$g_T = -(C'R_TC)^{-1}C'R_T(b - a_T). \tag{3.10}$$

Under optimal control the state variable x_T will be determined by

$$x_T = Ax_{T-1} + Cu_{T-1} + b = (A + CG_T)x_{T-1} + Cg_T + b. \tag{3.11}$$

Given (3.11) and (3.6) the optimum solution for the optimum Lagrange multiplier as a function of the state variable x_T is

$$\lambda_T = R_T(x_T - a_T) = R_T((A + CG_T)x_{T-1} + Cg_T + b - a_T)$$
$$= H_T x_{T-1} + h_T. \tag{3.12}$$

where we have defined

$$H_T = R_T(A + CG_T), \qquad (3.13)$$

$$h_T = R_T(Cg_T + b - a_T). \qquad (3.14)$$

The next step is to take as given functions the solutions (3.8) for $u_{T-1} = u_{T-1}(x_{T-1})$ and (3.12) for $\lambda_T = \lambda_T(x_{T-1})$ for the last period T and to solve the problem for the last two periods with the Lagrangean

$$L_2 = \beta^{T-1}(x_{T-1} - a_{T-1})' R_{T-1}(x_{T-1} - a_{T-1})/2$$
$$- \beta^{T-1}\lambda'_{T-1}[x_{T-1} - b - Ax_{T-2} - Cu_{T-2}]$$
$$- \beta^T \lambda'_T[x_T - b - (A + CG_T)x_{T-1} - Cg_t]. \qquad (3.15)$$

Note that the value of the objective function $\beta^T (x_T - a_T)' R_T(x_T - a_T)$ for the last period T has been maximized by choosing the optimum control function $u_{T-1} = u_{T-1}(x_{T-1})$ for u_{T-1}. The remaining problem is to choose u_{T-2} to maximize this two-period objective function. Another way to put it is that if we set up a Lagrangean involving the utility for the last two periods and try to find its maximum by differentiating with respect to u_{T-1}, x_T, u_{T-2} and x_{T-1}, the first-order conditions obtained for the first two derivatives are now solved. The remaining problem is to obtain and solve the first-order conditions from the second two derivatives.

Setting to zero the partial derivatives of L_2 with respect to u_{T-2} and x_{T-1}, respectively, gives

$$C'\lambda_{T-1} = 0, \qquad (3.16)$$

$$R_{T-1}(x_{T-1} - a_{T-1}) - \lambda_{T-1} + \beta(A + CG_T)'\lambda_T = 0, \qquad (3.17)$$

which correspond to (3.5) and (3.6). Pre-multiplying (3.17) by C' to make its second term equal to zero and using (3.12) to substitute for λ_T we obtain

$$C'R_{T-1}(x_{T-1} - a_{T-1}) + \beta C'(A + CG_T)'(H_T x_{T-1} + h_T)$$
$$= [C'R_{T-1} + \beta C'(A + CG_T)'H_T](Ax_{T-2} + Cu_{T-2} + b)$$
$$- C'R_{T-1}a_{T-1} + \beta C'(A + CG_T)'h_T$$

$$= [C'R_{T-1} + \beta C'(A + CG_T)'H_T]Ax_{T-2}$$
$$+ [C'R_{T-1} + \beta C'(A + CG_T)'H_T]Cu_{T-2}$$
$$+ [C'R_{T-1} + \beta C'(A + CG_T)'H_T]b - C'R_{T-1}a_{T-1}$$
$$+ \beta C'(A + CG_T)'h_T = 0$$

Solving this equation for u_{T-2} as a function of x_{T-2}, we get

$$u_{T-2} = -[C'R_{T-1}C + \beta C'(A + CG_T)'H_TC]^{-1}$$
$$\times \{[C'R_{T-1}A + \beta C'(A + CG_T)'H_TA]x_{T-2}$$
$$+ [C'R_{T-1} + \beta C'(A + CG_T)'H_T]b - C'R_{T-1}a_{T-1}$$
$$+ \beta C'(A + CG_T)'h_T]\}$$
$$= G_{T-1}x_{T-2} + g_{T-1}, \tag{3.18}$$

where

$$G_{T-1} = -[C'R_{T-1}C + \beta C'(A + CG_T)'H_TC]^{-1}$$
$$\times \{[C'R_{T-1}A + \beta C'(A + CG_T)'H_TA], \tag{3.19}$$
$$g_{T-1} = -[C'R_{T-1}C + \beta C'(A + CG_T)'H_TC]^{-1}$$
$$\times \{[C'R_{T-1} + \beta C'(A + CG_T)'H_T]b$$
$$- C'R_{T-1}a_{T-1} + \beta C'(A + CG_T)'h_T. \tag{3.20}$$

Equation (3.18) is the optimum control equation for u_{T-2} analogous to Equation (3.8).

As before under optimum control x_{T-2} will be determined by the equation

$$x_{T-1} = Ax_{T-2} + Cu_{T-2} + b = (A + CG_{T-1})x_{T-2} + Cg_{T-1} + b.$$

To find the optimum λ_{T-1} we use (3.17) and (3.12)

$$\lambda_{T-1} = R_{T-1}(x_{T-1} - a_{T-1}) + \beta(A + CG_T)'(H_Tx_{T-1} + h_T)$$
$$= [R_{T-1} + \beta(A + CG_T)'H_T]x_{T-1}$$
$$- R_{T-1}a_{T-1} + \beta(A + CG_T)'h_T$$

$$= [R_{T-1} + \beta(A + CG_T)'H_T][(A + CG_{T-1})x_{T-2} + Cg_{T-1} + b]$$

$$- R_{T-1}a_{T-1} + \beta(A + CG_T)'h_T$$

$$= H_{T-1}x_{T-2} + h_{T-1}, \tag{3.21}$$

where

$$H_{T-1} = [R_{T-1} + \beta(A + CG_T)'H_T](A + CG_{T-1}). \tag{3.22}$$

$$h_{T-1} = [R_{T-1} + \beta(A + CG_T)'H_T](Cg_{T-1} + b)$$

$$- R_{T-1}a_{T-1} + \beta(A + CG_T)'h_T. \tag{3.23}$$

To continue with this procedure, we maximize the objective function for the last three periods by forming a Lagrangean L_3 including the utility of period $T-2$ and differentiating it with respect to u_{T-3} and x_{T-2} and so forth. The time subscripts of all equations from (3.15) to (3.23) will be reduced by 1. By this process we complete the solution to the optimal control problem of finding the optimum feedback control function $u_t = G_{t+1}x_t + g_{t+1}$ for $t = T - 1, T - 2, \ldots, 0$ and the associated Lagrange function $\lambda_t = H_t x_{T-1} + h_t$ for $t = T, T - 1, \ldots, 1$ backward in time. To do so, we solve a set of equations for the matrices G_t and the vectors g_t and an associated set for H_t and h_t. For the last period G_T and g_T are given by (3.9) and (3.10), and H_T and h_T are given by (3.13) and (3.14). For the period $T - 1, G_{T-1}$ and g_{T-1} are given by (3.19) and (3.20) and H_{T-1} and h_{T-1} are given by (3.22) and (3.23). For any earlier period t, the last four equations remain valid with $T - 1$ replaced by t. The process continues until the optimal control rule for u_0 is found for the determination of x_1. The Equations (3.19), (3.20), (3.22) and (3.23) are known as matrix Ricatti equations in control theory. In this calculation we treat as given the parameters R_t and a_t of the utility function, A, C and b of the dynamic model and the discount rate β.

The formulation of the dynamic optimization problem as given by the Lagrangean expression (3.3) can accommodate the inclusion of both state and control variables in previous periods in the quadratic utility function and a higher order dynamic equation explaining x_{t+1} by the state and control variables further back in time. This is done by redefining the state variable. To illustrate consider the following dynamic equation

$$x_t = A_1 x_{t-1} + A_2 x_{t-2} + C_1 u_{t-1} + C_2 u_{t-2} + b. \qquad (3.24)$$

By redefining the state variable we can write it as the following first-order equation.

$$\begin{pmatrix} x_t \\ x_{t-1} \\ u_{t-1} \end{pmatrix} = \begin{pmatrix} A_1 & A_2 & C_2 \\ I & 0 & 0 \\ 0 & 0 & 0 \end{pmatrix} \begin{pmatrix} x_{t-1} \\ x_{t-2} \\ u_{t-2} \end{pmatrix} + \begin{pmatrix} C_1 \\ 0 \\ I \end{pmatrix} u_{t-1} + \begin{pmatrix} b \\ 0 \\ 0 \end{pmatrix}.$$

The above matrix equation can be redefined as $x_t = A x_{t-1} + C u_{t-1} + b$ for use in the Lagrangean expression (3.3). We can thus have both current and lagged state variables and control variables entering the utility function for determining the optimum path for CO_2 emission e_t. The redefinition of a vector of state variables to include these other variables can be useful in practical applications.

The above discussion deals only with a small part of the subject of optimal control or dynamic optimization. The dynamic model employed can be in discrete time or in continuous time. It may be deterministic or stochastic. We have dealt with only one deterministic control problem in discrete time. A different exposition of the method of this section was presented in Chow (1975, pp. 158–159). The steady state version of the matrix Ricatti equations was derived by the Lagrange method in Chow (1997, beginning with Section 2.3). Stochastic models in both discrete and continuous time are discussed in Chow (1997) where it is shown (in p. 145) that the Lagrange method for obtaining optimal feedback equations for stochastic models in continuous time is reduced to Pontryagin's maximum principle as a special case when the model becomes deterministic.

3.3. Optimum Path for CO_2 Emission Without Considering the Inertia of Change

We now solve the dynamic optimization problem specified by the Lagrangean expression (3.2). Differentiating the Lagrangean with respect to e_t and E_t respectively yields the following first order conditions. For any t,

$$\frac{1}{e_t} + \beta\lambda_{t+1}b_2 = 0 \quad \text{and} \quad -\frac{\theta}{M - E_t} + \beta\lambda_{t+1}b_1 - \lambda_t = 0.$$

Combining these two equations yields an equation explaining e_t by e_{t-1}

$$-\frac{\theta}{M - E_t} - \frac{b_1}{b_2}\frac{1}{e_t} + \frac{1}{\beta b_2 e_{t-1}} = 0,$$

which, together with the dynamic equation $E_{t+1} - b_1 E_t - b_2 e_t = 0$, determines the evolution of e_t and E_t. However, our solution may be questioned by those who conceive the problem for CO_2 emission as a problem of finding some optimal path for $e(t)$ from the present value of 8 to a steady state value for e that guarantees E to equal 600. They may ask how the optimum path of e_t obtained by solving our optimization problem will guarantee a steady state value of E equal to 600. We respond by challenging the premise of this question that the steady state of E has to be 600. Why not somewhat above or below 600? The above situation may mean more serious climate problems, but the world might accept the consequences if there are tremendous gains in output. Our viewpoint is that a steady state level for E close to 600 is justified only in the context of a solution to a dynamic optimization problem that allows for the proper balancing of the costs and benefits along the way and at the steady state. Consider again the above solution. In the steady state, we have $e_t = e$ and $E_t = E$. Letting $e_t = e$, $E_t = E$ and the using empirical values $b_1 = 0.9975$ and $b_2 = 0.5$ in the above two equations that determine the evolution of e_t and E_t, we obtain the steady state as follows,

$$e = \frac{1 - 0.9975\beta}{200(1 - 0.9975\beta) + 0.5\beta\theta}M \quad \text{and}$$

$$E = \frac{200(1 - 0.9975\beta)}{200(1 - 0.9975\beta) + 0.5\beta\theta}M.$$

Therefore, if the costs and benefits are described properly by our utility function we have shown that the optimal level of E is given by the equation above where M is the maximum tolerable value for

E and θ is a parameter in the utility function $\log(e) + \theta \log(M - E)$. The larger the value of θ the more we want the steady state value for E to be below M. If the steady state level of E turns out to be different from 600, it means either that the level 600 is not really the optimum, or that we have chosen incorrect parameter values for M and θ and should change them to reflect more accurately the tradeoff between more output and more CO_2 in the atmosphere. An advantage of our solution is that it takes into account the costs and benefits of emission in all future years up to time T.

From our approach to finding an optimum path of CO_2 emission through dynamic optimization, three comments can be made. First, while we consider global warming a serious problem we note that if we slow down the growth trend of emission in the near future, there is loss in output that is associated with the slow increase in e. No wonder some developing countries do not want to worry about controlling CO_2 emission today or in the near future in order to obtain more output. There will be time in the future to do so. For every year that these countries are asked to help control the emission of CO_2, they lose the benefit of more production and capital accumulation to enable them to have a developed economy.

Second, like many other recommendations for solving the global warming problem, the above solution has not allowed for the possibility of important technological innovations in the use of clean energy. If such innovations occur, efforts to reduce output today to solve the problem of global warming shall be regrettable. Without knowing the prospect of great innovations with regard to clean energy, one can point out that historically pessimists have often been wrong than right, beginning with the prediction by Malthus that food production could not catch up with the increase of population and famine would occur. Historically, food was produced mainly by the use of land and labor, and land was a limited resource just like natural resources in the discussion of environmental problems. Land as a resource was certainly limited in supply just like oil, and yet technological innovations have enabled the output of food per unit of land to increase many fold.

Third, the specific formulation of the optimal control problem as given by the Lagragian (3.2) can be improved to deal with possible inertia in changing the quantity of emission from year to year, or in changing the trend of emission, as will be discussed in the next section.

3.4. Accounting for the Inertia in the Quantity of Emission and in the Trend of Emission

To account for possible inertia in changing the amount of emission from year to year, and to ensure that the starting value of emission in the optimum path is not too far from the historical value in the previous year ($e = 8$ in our example), we can introduce a cost for changing the level of emission e each year. This is done by defining the change $c_t = e_t - e_{t-1}$ and incorporating this variable in the utility function as follows

$$\Sigma_1^T \{\beta^t[\log(e_t) + \beta\theta \log(M - E_{t+1}) - \tau c_t^2/2], \qquad (3.25)$$

The dynamic model for the state variable x_t is given by the following matrix equation

$$\begin{pmatrix} E_{t+1} \\ e_t \\ c_t \end{pmatrix} = \begin{pmatrix} b_1 & 0 & 0 \\ 0 & 0 & 0 \\ 0 & -1 & 0 \end{pmatrix} \begin{pmatrix} E_t \\ e_{t-1} \\ c_{t-1} \end{pmatrix} + \begin{pmatrix} b_2 \\ 1 \\ 1 \end{pmatrix} e_t$$

The vector of state variables so defined includes all variables in the above utility function and the algorithm of Section 3.2 can be applied after this utility function is approximated by a quadratic utility function, or after the derivative of this utility function is linearized. The dynamic model becomes a first-order system in the form to be used in the Lagrangean expression (3.3), the vector Lagrangean multiplier λ having three components.

In the notation of our algorithm, the derivative of the utility function is $R(x_t - a_t)$. In the notation of (3.25) the derivatives of the utility function with respect to the vector $x' = (E_{t+1}, e_t, c_t)$ are $(-\beta\theta(M - E_{t+1})^{-1}, e_t^{-1}, -\tau c_t)$. We linearize $-\beta\theta(M - E_{t+1})^{-1}$ about E^* (which is close to 200 when t is small and close to 600 when t is close to T) to get $-\beta\theta(M - E^*)^{-1} - \beta\theta(M - E^*)^{-2}(E_{t+1} - E^*)$. We linearize e_t^{-1} about e^* (which is close to 8 when t is small and close to 3 when t is close to T) to get $e_t^{*-1} - e_t^{*-2}(e_t - e_t^*)$. Using these derivatives but getting rid of the constant terms, we can write $R(x_t - a_t)$ as

$$
\begin{pmatrix} -\beta\theta(M - E^*)^{-2} & 0 & 0 \\ 0 & -e^{*-2} & 0 \\ 0 & 0 & -\tau \end{pmatrix} \begin{pmatrix} E_{t+1} - E^* \\ e_t - e^* \\ c_{t-1} - 0 \end{pmatrix}
$$

Now we have a quadratic utility function and a linear dynamic model to be used to find the optimum path of CO_2 emission e_t using the algorithm of Section 3.2.

To ensure that the initial e_1 for the determination of E_2 is close to 8 we can further introduce a target a_1 with its second component equal to 8 and apply some severe penalty in the second diagonal element of the matrix R_1 to prevent large deviation from 8. We can introduce the second difference or the rate of change in c_t which equals $s_t = c_t - c_{t-1}$ as given in the model below to ensure that the path of e_t does not decrease immediately at the beginning because of the momentum of the past increasing trend.

$$
\begin{pmatrix} E_{t+1} \\ e_t \\ c_t \\ s_t \end{pmatrix} = \begin{pmatrix} b_1 & 0 & 0 & 0 \\ 0 & 0 & 0 & 0 \\ 0 & -1 & 0 & 0 \\ 0 & -1 & -1 & 0 \end{pmatrix} \begin{pmatrix} E_t \\ e_{t-1} \\ c_{t-1} \\ s_{t-1} \end{pmatrix} + \begin{pmatrix} b_2 \\ 1 \\ 1 \\ 1 \end{pmatrix} e_t
$$

3.5. Numerical Solutions to the Optimal Path for CO_2 Emission

We now consider the numerical solution of the dynamic optimization problem represented by the Lagrange expression (3.25). One problem is to find an optimum path of CO_2 emission e beginning with the current value of 8 to reach a steady state given by Section 3.3 with the corresponding E beginning with the current level of 200. Illustrative numerical solutions to the optimum path e_t of CO_2 emission and the associated value for E_t for selected values of the parameters β, θ and M are given below.

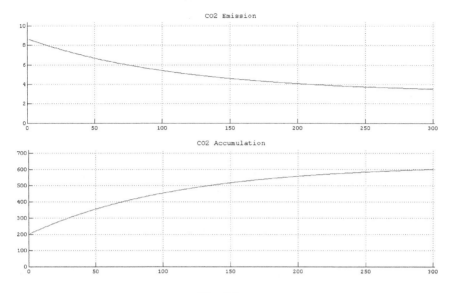

Fig. 3.1.

I present below illustrative numerical solutions for the optimum path e_t^* of CO_2 emission and the associated accumulation path E_t^* for selected values of the parameters β, M, θ and τ. For $\beta = 0.98, M = 800, \theta = 2.4$ and $\tau = 0$, Figure 3.1 shows both the optimal paths for e_t and E_t. Note that the initial e_t may differ from the current observed value 8 because we do not penalize the annual change in e_t by setting the value of τ equal to zero in the Lagrange expression L. The optimum path of e in Figure 3.1 is different from being a straight line downward and drops faster at the beginning than a straight line because a discount factor less than 1 makes the present reduction in e worth more than future reductions.

If β is reduced from 0.98 to 0.97 the future will become less important. The present reduction in e becomes steeper as shown in Figure 3.2.

In order to insure that the initial value of e be close to the historical value 8 and to demonstrate that the path can start by increasing first before declining, we set $e_0 = 8$, $\beta = 0.98$, $M = 800$, $\theta = 5.5$ and $\tau = 0.3$. The result is given in Figure 3.3. The result shows that the optimal path will begin with a value close to 8. Furthermore, the

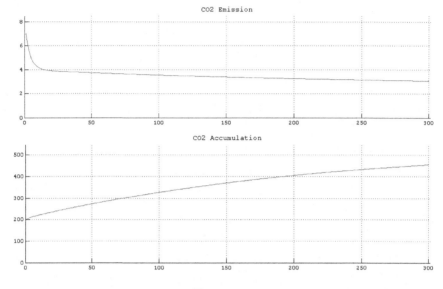

Fig. 3.2.

optimum path of e begins by increasing even when we give a high value for θ in the second term $\theta \log(M - E)$ of the utility function. We do not mind too much the damage of increasing e because E is still very far from an intolerable M. In the mean time we benefit from increasing output.

I am indebted to Jean-Francois Kagy for performing the calculation of the optimum paths displayed in Figures 3.1 to 3.3.

3.6. Comparison with the Socolow–Lam Optimum Path

Socolow and Lam (2006) presented an optimum path for CO_2 emission for the years 2005 onward that begins at the current observed value of 8 and reaches a steady state value of 3, such that the maximum change in e_t in any period is minimized. This implies that the rate of reduction in e_t must be constant. Hence, the emission path from $e_0 = 8$ to the steady-state value $e_T = 3$ must be a straight line because any deviation from a straight line would cause the rate of reduction to be larger than the minimum achievable (see Figure 3.7 in Socolow and Lam, 2006).

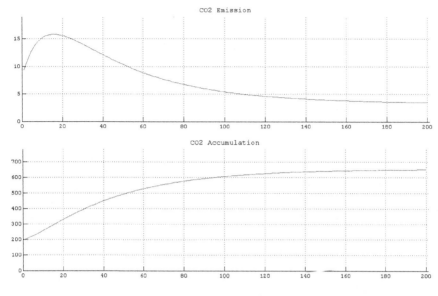

Fig. 3.3.

The approach to solving the CO$_2$ reduction problem presented in this chapter differs from the Socolow--Lam solution by considering the cost and benefit of both quantities e_t and E_t in each period along the way towards the steady state. We found that the optimal path of e_t may not be a downward sloping straight line, as in the Socolow-Lam solution. Furthermore, there is no guarantee that the steady-state value of E has to be 600. In our solution the steady-state value of E depends on the parameters of the objective function and can be somewhat below 600 or perhaps above it, depending crucially on the value of M and other parameters in the utility function. In other words, the approach presented in this paper takes into account the economics of the problem in all periods and is flexible by allowing the specification of different utility functions to reflect a set of assumptions chosen by the policy maker.

3.7. Concluding Comments

We begin this chapter by referring to a UN Climate Change Conference to discuss an optimum path for future CO$_2$ emission. This chapter will have no relevance if no consensus can be reached. If a consensus can be reached, this chapter may be useful in providing a framework under which the consensus can be summarized by a utility function for the world community and an optimum path for CO_2 emission can be found.

It may be suggested that a consensus is unlikely because different nations have different utility functions. For example the utility function of the developing nations will have a smaller value for θ, giving less importance to the harm of global warming than the increase in output. Such a situation can be studied by postulating two sets of nations, the developing and the developed, as players of a two person dynamic game, each having its utility function and the action e_{it} of player i affects the utility of player j because

$$E_t = 0.9975E_{t-1} + 0.5(e_{1t} + e_{2t}).$$

Each will solve its own dynamic optimization problem as suggested in this chapter with its optimum control path for e_{it} depending on e_{jt}.

It is also suggested that uncertainty regarding the size of the damage of climate change makes the discussion more complicated than suggested in this chapter in which the disutility of a large E is known and given in the utility function. (See the references by Nordhaus 2007, 2008, Stern 2007, Weitzman 2007, Zedillo 2008 and Dyson 2008). That general discussion even raises the question as to whether we should devote resources to mitigate climate change at all. The present chapter assumes that we have sufficient knowledge as given by the model and will devote resources to mitigate climate change by reducing e for the benefit of production and at the same time increasing utility from its second term $\theta \log(M - E_t)$. We have tried to answer the question as to how much resource in terms of the reduction in output should be devoted to the reduction of carbon emission.

References

Chow, Gregory C. (1975). *Analysis and Control of Dynamic Economic Systems*. New York: John Wiley and Sons.

Chow, G. C. (1997). *Dynamic Economics: Optimization by the Lagrange Method*. Oxford: Oxford University Press.

Kolstad C. and Toman M. (2005). "The Economics of Climate Policy," in Maler K., Vincent J. (ed) *Handbook of Environmental Economics*, vol 3. North–Holland, Amsterdam.

Dyson, F. (2008). The Question of Global Warming. *New York Times Review of Books*. No. 10, Vol. 55, June 12.

Nordhaus, W. D. (2007). "A Review of the Stern Review on the Economics of Climate Change," *Journal of Economic Literature*, Vol. XLV (September), pp. 686–702.

Nordhaus, W. D. (2008). *A Question of Balance: Weighing the Options on Global Warming Policies*. Yale University Press.

Stern, N. (2007). *The Economics of Climate Change: The Stern Review*. Cambridge and New York: Cambridge University Press.

Socolow, Robert and Lam, S. H. (2006). "Good Enough Tools for Global Warming Policy Making," *Philosophical Transactions of Royal Society A*, pp. 1–38.

Weitzman, M. L. (2007). "A Review of the Stern Review on the Economics of Climate Change," *Journal of Economic Literature*, Vol. XLV (September), pp. 703–724.

Zedillo, E., ed. (2008). *Global Warming: Looking Beyond Kyoto*. Yale Center for the Study of Globalization/Brookings Institution Press.

Chapter 4
Macroeconomic Models Incorporating the Effect of Pollution

4.1. Introduction

In this chapter, I propose two models incorporating the consideration of pollution to explain certain aspects of the Chinese macroeconomic economy.[1] The first treats pollution as a byproduct of macroeconomic production by the simple assumption that pollution is proportional to output, as will be discussed in Section 4.2. A main motivation for discussing this model is that it helps to pinpoint clearly the issue of sustainable development. In Section 4.3, I present results from empirical estimation and testing of the model of Section 4.2 using Chinese data. A measure of Green GDP will be provided. The model explains the decline in the rate of consumption growth in recent years but fails to explain the prospect of continued growth in the Chinese macroeconomy. Section 4.4 shows that a market economy with consumers maximizing utility and producers maximizing profits will yield the same theory as the one in Section 4.2, which was derived from maximization by an all-knowing central planner. A second model in Section 4.5 assumes a different utility function with cumulative emission E as an argument and without setting an upper limit M for emission. It also includes emission e as a factor of production. Chinese data are used to test this relation in Section 4.6 with encouraging results. Section 4.7 shows that the model of Section 4.5 can also be obtained by a market solution. The effect of market failure in the regulation of pollution is treated in Section 4.8.

---

[1]For a survey on how pollution or the environmental good is associated with preference and production in macroeconomic models, see Xepapsdeas (2005, Section 2).

4.2.   A Macroeconomic Model Assuming Pollution to be Proportional to Output

A macroeconomic model can serve two purposes. In the realm of positive economics, it is constructed to explain macroeconomic phenomena. In normative economics, it can be used to provide policy recommendations to improve economic performance. If one believes in the working of Adam Smith's invisible hand, one can construct the same model of a market economy which is both descriptive of reality and shows how efficient allocation of resources is achieved. Assuming that the market solution is efficient, economists have constructed macroeconomic models to explain reality by an optimization exercise. In this exercise, a social objective function is defined and an all-knowing central planner is assumed to solve an optimization problem to maximize an objective function. The implications of the solution are interpreted as propositions concerning the behavior of the actual macroeconomy. This approach fails if the market does not work perfectly or does not allocate resources efficiently, as in the case of allocating natural resources. Even in this case it is a useful exercise to construct a macroeconomic model under the assumption of market efficiency and then introduce market failure to improve its power for explaining observed phenomena. Performing this exercise, we obtain an understanding of how an actual inefficient market works and how it can be made to work better. This is the methodology that I follow in this chapter.

In this section, I build a macroeconomic model under the assumption that the market economy in China is efficient and use it to describe the Chinese macroeconomy and to explain Chinese macroeconomic data. This model is constructed by assuming that a central planner is maximizing an objective function for China. Deriving a macroeconomic model for China by optimization has had a long history, including the work of Chow and Kwan (1996), among others.

In our model we assume a Cobb–Douglas production function $Y_t = a_t K_t^\gamma L_t^{1-\gamma}$ where a_t, K_t, and L_t denote, respectively, total factor productivity in period t, capital stock at the beginning of period t and labor in period t. As is fairly customary in macroeconomic modeling the economy is composed of a number of representative consumers and the same number of representative firms. This construction assumes away the problem of aggregating the behavior of heterogeneous consumers and firms but has been found useful in modeling certain important features of a macroeconomy. It enables us to use the same symbol to denote a variable for one consumer, one producer or for the aggregate economy.

I begin by assuming that a central planner maximizes a utility function in each period t subject to a budget constraint: national saving $K_{t+1} - (1 - d)K_t$, d being the rate of depreciation of the capital stock at the beginning of period t, equals income Y_t minus consumption C_t. For each period t, this constraint for K_{t+1} is introduced by using a Lagrange multiplier λ_{t+1} to form a Lagrange expression as given below. The utility function is $\log C_t + \theta \log(M - e_t)$ where e_t denotes emission or pollution in period t and M is the maximum amount of pollution that can be tolerated. It thus has two parameters θ and M, with θ measuring the relative importance of clean environment $(M - e)$ as compared with consumption. In Chapter 1, we assumed output Y to be generated by a Cobb–Douglas production function $a_t K_t^\gamma L_t^{1-\gamma} e^\delta$, with emission e as a factor of production. In this section, we choose a different production function by assuming emission to be proportional to output, namely, $e_t = cY_t$, and $Y_t = a_t K_t^\gamma L_t^{1-\gamma}$. If $e_t = cY_t$ and e_t cannot exceed M, this model shows how emission can prevent sustainable economic development.

The problem of the central planner is to maximize the sum of discounted future utilities in all future periods subject to the above constraint for each period, β being the discount factor. The first-order condition for maximum can be obtained by differentiating the Lagrange expression (4.1) below with respect to the control variable C_t and the state variable K_t for each period t, noting that Y is a function of K.

$$L = \sum_t \beta^t \{[\log C_t + \theta \log(M - e_t)]$$
$$- \beta \lambda_{t+1}[K_{t+1} - (1 - d)K_t - Y_t + C_t]\}. \tag{4.1}$$

Differentiation of (4.1) with respect to the control variable C_t and the state variable K_t for each period t yields

$$C_t^{-1} = \beta\lambda_{t+1}, \tag{4.2}$$

$$-\theta\gamma e_t K_t^{-1}/(M - e_t) - \lambda_t + (1 - d)\beta\lambda_{t+1} + \gamma YK^{-1}\beta\lambda_{t+1} = 0. \tag{4.3}$$

Using (4.2) to substitute C for λ in (4.3) gives

$$-\theta\gamma e_t K_t^{-1}/(M - e_t) - \beta^{-1}C_{t-1}^{-1} + C_t^{-1}[(1 - d) + \gamma YK^{-1}] = 0, \tag{4.4}$$

which can be rewritten as

$$C_t = [1 - d + \gamma YK^{-1}]/[\theta\gamma e_t K_t^{-1}/(M - e_t) + \beta^{-1}C_{t-1}^{-1}]. \tag{4.5}$$

If the pollution term does not appear in the utility function or if $\theta = 0$, Equation (4.5) will be reduced to

$$C_t = [1 - d + \gamma Y_t K_t^{-1}]\beta C_{t-1}. \tag{4.6}$$

Let us examine whether this model without pollution can explain the evolution of consumption in China. Empirically, the ratio of output Y to capital K for China has a mean of 0.2768 for the period 1978–2005 (See Table 4.2). If γ is about 0.6 and d is 0.04 (see Chow (2015, Chapter 5) for estimates of γ and the depreciation rate d), the coefficient in square brackets on the right-hand side of (4.6) is $0.96 + 0.6$ times $0.2768 = 1.126$. The annual discount factor β has to be as low as 0.95 to make the annual growth rate of consumption equal to 7.0% to match the mean annual growth rate during the period 1997–2007 as given in Table 4.2. Equation (4.5) incorporating the effect of pollution can match the decreasing rate of consumption growth during this period much better as explained in the first point below.

I would like to draw three important economic implications from this model of pollution as stated in Equation (4.5).

First, if the disutility of pollution does not matter or if $\theta = 0$, Equation (4.5) is reduced to Equation (4.6). Since the contribution of the pollution term in the denominator of Equation (4.5) is positive, the disutility of pollution makes consumption smaller than it would be otherwise. To put this point in terms of the ratio C_t/C_{t-1} we divide both sides of Equation (4.5) by C_{t-1} to obtain

$$C_t/C_{t-1} = [1 - d + \gamma YK^{-1}]/[\theta\gamma e_t C_{t-1} K_t^{-1}/(M - e_t) + \beta^{-1}].$$
$$(4.7)$$

Equation (4.7) shows that the rate of growth of consumption is made smaller than otherwise by the positive pollution term $\theta\gamma e_t C_{t-1} K_t^{-1}/(M - e_t)$ in its denominator if we assume the ratio Y/K in its numerator to be given. In the course of economic development, there is a tendency for this pollution term in the denominator to increase because of the increase in e, unless this effect is somehow offset by a reduction of the ratio C_{t-1}/K_t. The data for China to be presented in the next section will show that the ratio C_t/C_{t-1} has been indeed declining. Our model provides an explanation of this decline, although there are other reasonable models that can also provide an explanation.

Second, because e_t cannot exceed the limit M, under the assumption $Y_t = e_t/c$, Y_t cannot exceed M/c. Thus economic growth eventually stops according to this model, unless we revise this assumption and allow technological innovation to lower the ratio e_t/Y_t. In the framework of this model, economic development can be sustained only by solving the environmental problems, or by reducing the ratio $c = e/Y$ so as not to allow e to reach the limit M. Thus this model pinpoints the importance of controlling pollution for sustainable economic development.

Third, this model provides a measure of the disutility of pollution associated with a given increase in consumption, as given by the utility function for specific values of the parameters θ and M. This measure is related to the measurement of Green GDP. The latter nets out from GDP the cost of productive resources used to repair the damage to the environment. Green GDP has limited use because knowing the cost of repairing environmental damage in the production of a given amount of output one still does not know whether the environmental cost is worth paying for. Our measure nets out the disutility of a polluted environment from the utility derived from consuming a given output. Our framework can be used to measure the change in net utility when consumption changes from C_1 to C_2 while pollution changes from e_1 to e_2. To do so we compute $\log C_2 + \theta \log(M - e_2) - [\log C_1 + \theta \log(M - e_1)]$. This change has not yet allowed for the discount factor if the change is from one period to another rather than from one hypothetical output-pollution combination to another for the same period.

4.3.   Estimation of the Macromodel Incorporating Pollution for China

Table 4.1 provides data on China's air pollution from 1997 to 2006. The first row of the Table shows that in 1997 the index of Industrial Waste Air Emission was 113375 and in 2006 it has increased to 330992.

The other macroeconomic data used in our statistical analysis are given in Table 4.2.

Real GDP is denoted by Y, capital stock by K, consumption in constant prices by C and industrial waste air pollution by e, the values of which are given on the first row of Table 4.1 from 1997 to 2006 and, for the years before 1997, approximately estimated by multiplying y by 5.5419, the mean of the ratios e/Y for the years 1997–2006 (Y in 2006 not shown in Table 4.2). Data on Y and C are official data from *China Statistical Yearbook* 2006. Data on K are from Chow (2015), updated by the same method as described on page 96 of that book and converted to 1978 prices to conform to data for Y and C.

The data in Table 4.2 are used to estimate Equation (4.5) rewritten below:

$$C_t = [1 - d + \gamma Y K^{-1}]/[\theta \gamma e_t K_t^{-1}/(M - e_t) + \beta^{-1} C_{t-1}^{-1}]. \quad (4.5)$$

For the purpose of estimation, the values of d and γ are assumed to be 0.04 and 0.60, respectively, from our knowledge of these parameters; the value of β^{-1} is assumed to be 1.02 as the value of the discount factor β is often assumed to be 0.98. Only the parameters M and θ in Equation (4.5) are required to be estimated. We first use the sample from 1997 to 2005 when data on pollution are available as given in Table 4.2. For different assumed values of M, the first

Table 4.1.   Data on air pollution in China.

		1997	1998	1999	2000	2001	2002	2003	2004	2005	2006
Industrial Waste Air Emission[1]	100 million cu.m	113375	121203	126807	138145	160863	175257	198906	237696	268988	330992
Fuels Burning	100 million cu.m	70918	72985	75919	81970	93526	103776	116447	139726	155238	181636
Production Process	100 million cu.m	42457	48218	50887	56032	67337	71481	82459	97971	113749	149353
Sulfur Dioxide Emission	10 000 tons	2346	2090	1857	1995	1948	1927	2159	2255	2549	2589
Industrial[2]	10 000 tons	1852	1593	1460	1612	1567	1562	1792	1891	2168	2235
Non-Industrial[3]	10 000 tons	494	497	397	383	381	365	367	364	381	354
Soot Emission	10 000 tons	1873	1452	1159	1165	1070	1013	1049	1095	1183	1089
Industrial[4]	10 000 tons	1565	1175	953	953	852	804	846	887	949	864
Non-Industrial[5]	10 000 tons	308	277	206	212	218	209	202	209	234	224

(*Continued*)

Table 4.1. (*Continued*)

		1997	1998	1999	2000	2001	2002	2003	2004	2005	2006
Industrial Dust Emission[6]	10 000 tons	1505	1322	1175	1092	991	941	1021	905	911	808

[1] Industrial Waste Air Emission refers to the discharge into atmosphere of waste air containing pollutants generated from fuel burning and production processes in enterprises within a given period of time. It is calculated at standard status (273 K, 101 325 Pa).

[2] Sulfur Dioxide Emission through Industrial Activities refers to volume of sulphur dioxide emission from fuel burning and production process by enterprises during a given period of time.

[3] Sulfur Dioxide Emission through Non-industrial and Other Activities is calculated on the basis of consumption of coal by households and other activities and the sulphur content of coal.

[4] Industrial Soot Emission refers to the volume of soot in smoke emitted in the process of fuel burning in the premises of enterprises.

[5] Soot Emission by Consumption and Others refers to the net volume of soot emitted by fuel burning from all social and economic activities and operations of public facilities other than industrial activities. It is calculated on the basis of coal consumption by households and others.

[6] Industrial Dust Emission refers to volume of dust emitted by production process of enterprises and suspended in the air for a given period of time, including dust from refractory material of iron and steel works, dust from coke-screening systems and sintering machines of coke plants, dust from lime kilns and dust from cement production in building material enterprises, but excluding soot and dust emitted from power plants.

Note: I thank Dr. Wang Yi of the People's Bank of China for supplying these data to me. (In China, all data on environment are investigated and collected by National Bureau of Environment. The National Development and Reform Commission and National Bureau of Statistics all rely on these data from the National Bureau of Environment.)

Table 4.2.   Macroeconomic Data of China.

Year	Y	K	C	e
1978	3645.22	13910.7	2239.1	20201.34
1979	3922.25	14769.03	2542.7	21736.6
1980	4228.45	15746.23	2798	23433.53
1981	4450.81	16691.12	3058.6	24665.81
1982	4851.78	17816.94	3385.7	26887.94
1983	5380.34	19160.45	3723.4	29817.15
1984	6196.87	20709.59	4166.4	34342.25
1985	7031.62	22709.03	4668.7	38968.33
1986	7654.96	24961.7	5082.2	42422.8
1987	8540.74	27470.07	5527.8	47331.68
1988	9503.08	30686.13	6216	52664.84
1989	9889.48	34351.8	6497.5	54806.23
1990	10268.58	37781.34	6650.6	56907.14
1991	11212.69	41306.76	7254.2	62139.29
1992	12809.29	45441.53	8184.8	70987.43
1993	14595.45	51172.44	9046.2	80886.1
1994	16505.54	57508.32	10014.1	91471.57
1995	18309.93	64716.96	11067.9	101471.3
1996	20143.47	72516.72	12429.5	111632.5
1997	22013.47	80523.36	13419	113375
1998	23737.66	88879.67	14508.9	121203
1999	25549.33	97719.5	15851.2	126807
2000	27700.01	106568	17174.8	138145
2001	30000.14	116207.5	18297	160863
2002	32726.76	126940.3	19497.8	175257
2003	36007.46	139605.6	20532.3	198906
2004	39638.09	153682.1	21577.8	237696
2005	43695.22	168794.5	23130.6	268988

three rows of Table 4.3 give estimates of θ obtained by the nonlinear regression routine of STATA, together with its t statistic, root mean square error and R-square of the regression. All estimates of θ are highly significant and the values of R-square are very high. Note

Table 4.3.   Regressions to explain consumption by Equation (4.5).

Period	$1 - d$	M	θ	t statistic	R-squared	Root MSE
1997–2005	0.96	1000000	0.7468209	7.12	0.9999	188.9336
1997–2005	0.96	10000000	9.345796	7.37	0.9999	183.2962
1997–2005	0.96	1100000	0.8430062	7.16	0.9999	187.9435
1978–2005	0.9958	1100000	1.965221	13.35	0.9996	232.4537
1978–2005	0.96	90000000	85.72903	7.38	0.9998	183.1053
1978–2005	0.96	1100000	0.814789	7.29	0.9998	183.3053
1978–2005	0.96	1000000	0.7226108	7.28	0.9998	183.4771
1978–2005	0.96	10000000	8.95161	7.31	0.9998	182.9961
1997–2005	0.95850	1000000	0.6802665	2.47	0.9998	187.0087

that the value of θ increases as M increases. The reason is that for a larger M, the percentage change of $(M - e)$ is smaller for the same change in e; this requires a larger value of θ to yield the same percentage change in the term $\theta \log(M - e)$ in the utility function. When we vary the value of M substantially, the goodness of fit of the regression as measured by the RMSE remains almost the same. This fact is consistent with the fact that if we try to estimate both θ and M simultaneously, the standard errors of both are very large or we cannot obtain reasonably accurate estimates of both parameters. In any case, the positive and highly significant estimates of θ supports strongly our model of pollution. Our theory of pollution would be rejected if the estimates of θ were statistically insignificant, and Equation (4.5) would be reduced to Equation (4.6). I have tried to estimate both parameters d and θ, given the value of M, and found that the estimate of d is almost exactly equal to 0.04 and that the estimate of θ remains almost the same.

I have also tried to estimate Equation (4.5) using a longer sample period from 1978 to 2005. To do so, data for e before 1997 have been constructed by multiplying Y by 5.5419, the mean of the ratios C/Y for the years 1997–2006 (Y in 2006 not shown in Table 3.2). As shown in the lower half of Table 4.3, all statements of the last paragraph remain valid for the larger sample.

After the successful estimation of the model using data for 1978 to 2005 it then occurred to me that the variable e in our utility function can be replaced by national output Y or any other variable proportional to it. To test this proposition, I used the sample from 1997 onward when the data on pollution are available and estimated Equation (4.5) after substituting Y for e. The result, for a given value of M equal to four times the value of Y in 2005 as $M = 1100000$ is about four times the value of e in 2005, is about as good as the model using e. The estimate of θ is 4.109, with a standard error of 0.570, and a t ratio of 7.21 while the Root MSE equals to 187.0105, which is about the same as given in the top half of Table 3.4, and R-square is 0.9999. Thus, if we let Y instead of e enter the utility function, we will find the estimate of the parameter θ to be equally good and the resulting equation to explain C equally well. As is often the case when a macroeconomic hypothesis is proposed, one finds the hypothesis to be sufficient in explaining the data but not necessary. There are alternative hypotheses that will explain the data equally well. For the purpose of examining the macroeconomic implication of pollution, we know that pollution is highly correlated with output Y. Hence it is difficult to distinguish between the effect of pollution and of other variables that are highly correlated with Y.

The failure of our model to distinguish between alternative variables to be used as e in our utility function as long as the variables are highly correlated makes our theoretical framework more general. Our general model implies that in the course of economic development, the increase in output enables the population to derive more utility from a higher level of consumption but the increase in output itself reduces utility because it produces more pollution, congestion, or whatever other negative side effect. Our utility function is identical with the formulation often used for the choice of labor hour where more labor or hours of work (corresponding to our variable e now interpreted as "effort") reduces utility and this effect is measured by the difference between a maximum amount and the actual amount e. An important finding of this chapter is that if pollution or any other variable related to the increase in output asserts a negative effect on utility, it should be incorporated in a macroeconomic model and such a model explains the Chinese macroeconomic data better than the one without using it. Although pollution is not a necessary explanation of our empirical results, incorporating it has implications supported by Chinese data. In the study of economic growth, we suggest the consideration of not only the positive effect of increased consumption but also the negative effect of any variable associated with the increase in output itself. We are led to this proposition by studying the disutility of pollution. (Pollution associated with consumption rather than output can be modeled in our framework by defining consumption as productive work by the consumer herself.)

Equation (4.7) shows how an increase in pollution contributes to a reduction in the rate of growth of consumption, or in the ratio C_t/C_{t-1}. If pollution is not modeled, the first term involving θ would disappear. The importance of this pollution term of the denominator on the right side is measured by its ratio to the second term β^{-1}. This ratio, with $\theta\gamma = 1.37655, M = 1200000$ and $\beta^{-1} = 1.02$, increases monotonically from 0.00338 in 1979 to 0.04984 in 2005 as the value of $(M - e)$ in the denominator of the first term decreases with the increase in emission e. Although the ratio is small, by 2005 it is about 5%. Thus, we find that the pollution term involving a non-zero θ reduces the ratio C_t/C_{t-1} by about 5% in 2005.

The second effect of the pollution term is on the numerator $[1 - d + 0.6Y/K]$ of the expression to explain the ratio C_t/C_{t-1}. The reduction in the ratio of C_t/C_{t-1} as pollution increases, which we pointed out in the last paragraph, will cause a larger fraction of output Y to be used for capital formation. This will lead to a reduction in $[1 - d + 0.6Y/K]$ in the numerator of the expression explaining the ratio C_t/C_{t-1}. This is an additional factor in explaining why damage to the environment would make economic growth unsustainable. Empirically, the ratio Y/K for China decreases almost monotonically from 0.311 in 1987 to 0.259 in 2005.

Measuring change of utility: $\log C_2 + \theta \log(M - e_2) - [\log C_1 + \theta \log(M - e_1)]$.

Given $M = 1,000,000$ and $\theta = 0.7468$ (see Table 4.3), the change of e from 56,907 in 1990 to 268,988 in 2005 (see Table 4.2) implies the change in utility due to this increase in pollution by the amount

$$0.7468[\log(1,000,000 - 268,988) - \log(1,000,000 - 56,907)]$$
$$= 0.7468[13.592 - 13.757] = -0.2442$$

During the same period, income Y increased from 10,269 to 43,695 (see Table 4.2). Given a log utility function, the increase in utility is

$$\log(43,695) - \log(10,269) = 1.4481.$$

Thus by the above utility function, from 1990 to 2005, the Chinese people considered the increase in utility due to the increase in income to be much greater than the loss of utility due to the increase in pollution. Using the second utility function reported in Table 4.3, the change in utility due to the increase in pollution during this period is

$$9.346[\log(10,000,000 - 268,988) - \log(10,000,000 - 56,907)]$$
$$= 9.346[16.0908 - 16.1124] = -0.2016$$

which is not far from previous estimate -0.2442.

4.4.   Market Solution of the Problem of Section 4.2

In this section, I will show that Equation (4.3) of Section 4.2 derived by the central planner maximizing utility subject to a dynamic constraint with respect to C_t and K_t can be derived in a market economy with consumers maximizing utility subject to a budget constraint and producers maximizing profits. If this is the case, the market economy is efficient, working as efficiently as a central planner who is all-knowing (knowing the representative consumer's utility function and the representative firm's production function).

The representative consumer owns capital stock equal to K, labor equal to L and the natural environment, which enables him to sell emission permits e. The return to capital is r; the wage rate is w and the price of emission permits is q. Thus his income is $Y = rK + wL + qe$. His control variables are C and e, and his state variable is K. We will keep e in the utility function and will not replace it by caK^γ as in case for the central planner of Section 3.2 because pollution is what the consumer cares about. We normalize the labor of the representative consumer by one.

The representative consumer maximizes the Lagrangean expression

$$L = \sum_t \{\beta^t [\log C_t + \theta \log(M - e_t)$$

$$- \beta^{t+1} \lambda_{t+1} [K_{t+1} - (1 - d)K_t - r_t K_t - q_t e_t - w_t + C_t]\},$$

with respect to C, e and K, yielding

$$C_t^{-1} = \beta \lambda_{t+1}, \tag{4.8}$$

$$\theta/(M - e_t) = q_t \beta \lambda_{t+1}, \tag{4.9}$$

$$\lambda_t = (1 - d + r_t)\beta \lambda_{t+1}. \tag{4.10}$$

Using (4.8) to replace $\beta \lambda_{t+1}$ by C_t^{-1} in (4.9) and (4.10), respectively, yields

$$\theta/(M - e_t) = q_t C_t^{-1}, \tag{4.11}$$

$$C_t = (1 - d + r_t)\beta C_{t-1} \tag{4.12}$$

Given C_{t-1}, Equation (4.12) determines C_t. Given C_t, Equation (4.11) determines the supply of e for a given price q. It is a supply equation for e and can be written as

$$(M - e_t) = (1 - d + r_t)\beta\theta/q_t. \tag{4.13}$$

This equation shows that the supply of emission permits e increases with price q.

For any period, the representative producer is assumed to maximize profit which equals

$$aK^\gamma L^{1-\gamma} - rK - wL - qe = aK^\gamma L^{1-\gamma} - rK - wL - qcaK^\gamma L^{1-\gamma}$$

$$= (1 - qc)aK^\gamma L^{1-\gamma} - rK - wL.$$

Differentiating with respect to K and L yields

$$r = (1 - qc)\gamma Y/K, \tag{4.14}$$

$$w = (1 - qc)(1 - \gamma)Y/L. \tag{4.15}$$

If q is known, these two demand equations for capital and labor determine r and w because the supply of K and L is given. The output Y is also given by the production function once K and L are given.

Substitute (4.14) for r in (4.10) yields

$$\lambda_t = (1 - d)\beta\lambda_{t+1} + (1 - ca_t)\gamma Y_t K_t^{-1}\beta\lambda_{t+1}$$
$$= (1 - d)\beta\lambda_{t+1} + \gamma Y_t K_t^{-1}\beta\lambda_{t+1} - cq_t\gamma Y_t K_t^{-1}\beta\lambda_{t+1}.$$

We use (4.9) to replace $q_t\beta\lambda_{t+1}$ by $\theta/(M - e_t)$ to obtain

$$\lambda_t = (1 - d)\beta\lambda_{t+1} + \gamma Y_t K_t^{-1}\beta\lambda_{t+1} - c\gamma Y_t K_t^{-1}\theta/(M - e_t),$$

which is the same equation as Equation (4.3) of Section 4.2 derived by the central planner maximizing his objective function with respect to the state variable K. This shows that the market economy is efficient. Equation (4.3) of Section 4.2 has yielded

$$-\theta\gamma c K_t^{-1}Y_t/(M - e) - \beta^{-1}C_{t-1}^{-1} + C_t^{-1}[(1 - d) + \gamma Y_t K_t^{-1}] = 0.$$

$$(4.4)$$

from which we have derived Equation (4.7) for the purpose of estimation.

Finally, we consider the determination of the price q and quantity e of emission permits by the supply from consumers and demand by producers. Under the assumption that the demand for emission is $e = cY$, the price q of emission permits is determined by using the supply Equation (4.13).

$$(M - e_t) = (1 - d + r_t)\beta\theta/q_t. \tag{4.13}$$

How can market failure be incorporated in this model? Let the consumer, or the central planner in the case of modeling by optimization on his part, undervalue the disutility of pollution or the utility of a clean environment. This is done by using a smaller value of the parameter θ in the second term $\theta\log(M - e)$ of the utility function. He allows himself to have more emission than the optimum amount relative to consumption. This would increase pollution e for a given output or consumption C according to the supply Equation (4.13) of pollution e. Once the supply of emission permits increases, the price of emission permits will be lower. The consumer will receive less income since the demand by the producer is fixed but the price is lower. The producer will receive a higher profit by paying less for the emission permits.

4.5.   A Second Model to Explain China's Pollution

There are two ways to treat pollution in a model of the macro-economy. The first is to treat it as a byproduct of production, and the second as a factor of production. The model of Section 4.2 treats pollution as a byproduct of production and assumes that pollution is proportional to output. In order to improve the explanation of pollution, this section treats pollution as a factor of production and assumes a Cobb–Douglas production function of the form

$$Y = AK^{\alpha}L^{1-\alpha}e^{\delta} \tag{4.16}$$

In addition, the utility function is changed to

$$\log(C_t - \theta E_{t+1}^{\gamma}) \tag{4.17}$$

To imbed the above utility function in a model for a macroeconomy under the control of a central planner, with cumulated pollution $E_{t+1} = E_t + b_2 e_t$, I form the Lagrangean

$$L = \sum_t \{\beta^t [\log(C_t - \theta E_{t+1}^{\gamma}) - \beta^{t+1}\lambda_{t+1}[K_{t+1} - (1-d)K_t - Y_t + C_t]$$

$$- \beta^{t+1}\mu_{t+1}[E_{t+1} - b_1 E_t - b_2 e_t]\}, \tag{4.18}$$

where θE_{t+1}^{γ} in the utility function will be reduced to θe_t^{γ} for the special case of $b_1 = 0$ and $b_2 = 1$.

Differentiating L with respect to C_t and K_t, recalling the Cobb–Douglas production function for Y in (4.16), yields the first-order conditions

$$(C_t - \theta E_{t+1}^{\gamma})^{-1} = \beta\lambda_{t+1} \tag{4.19}$$

$$\text{and} \quad \lambda_t = \beta[1 - d + \alpha Y_t K_t^{-1}]\lambda_{t+1}. \tag{4.20}$$

Differentiating L with respect to e_t and E_t, respectively, yields

$$\delta Y_t e_t^{-1} \lambda_{t+1} = -b_2 \mu_{t+1} \tag{4.21}$$

and $\quad \mu_t = -\beta^{-1}\theta\gamma(C_{t-1} - \theta E_t^\gamma)^{-1} E_t^{\gamma-1} + \beta b_1 \mu_{t+1}. \tag{4.22}$

Using (4.21) to replace μ_t and μ_{t+1} by functions of λ_t and λ_{t+1} in (4.22) and replacing the latter by the left-hand-side of (4.19) we have

$$b_2^{-1}\delta(C_{t-1} - \theta E_t^\gamma)^{-1}\beta^{-1}Y_{t-1}e_{t-1}^{-1}$$
$$= \beta^{-1}\theta\gamma(C_{t-1} - \theta E_t^\gamma)^{-1} E_t^{\gamma-1} + (C_t - \theta E_{t+1}^\gamma)^{-1} b_1 b_2^{-1}\delta Y_t e_t^{-1}. \tag{4.23}$$

In the special case when $b_1 = 0$ and $b_2 = 1$, (4.23) is reduced to

$$\delta Y_t = \theta\gamma e_t^\gamma. \tag{4.24}$$

Taking logarithm on both sides of (4.24) we have

$$\log(e_t) = \gamma^{-1}\log(\delta/\theta\gamma) + \gamma^{-1}\log(Y_t). \tag{4.25}$$

Equation (4.25) can be derived by replacing E_{t+1} by e_t in the utility function and deleting the second constraint in the Lagrangean (4.18) before solving the optimization problem. This positive relationship between $\log(e_t)$ and $\log(Y_t)$ is more reasonable than the assumption of the model of Section 4.2 that pollution is proportional to output. Given the parameters of the production function, the parameters θ and γ can be used to obtain a measure of "green" GDP by subtracting θe^γ from Y based on our utility function $\log(Y - \theta e^\gamma)$.

4.6. Using Our Macroeconomic Model to Explain Chinese Data

In this section, I use the model of Section 4.5 to explain Chinese data. Chinese pollution data are used to estimate Equation (4.25). Data on China's air pollution are given in Table 4.1. The first row of Table 4.1 shows that, in 2002, the index of Industrial Waste Air Emission was 175257 and in 2006 it increased to 330992. We will find

Table 4.4.   Output Y and its determinants K, L and t.

Year	GDP (at 1952 prices)	GDP (at 1978 prices)	K (at 1952 prices)	K (at 1978 prices)	L	t
1952	60.7	799.00	168.12	2213.00	20729	0
1953	68.9	911.00	180.88	2381.00	21364	0
1954	72.6	964.00	195.70	2576.00	21832	0
1955	77.4	1026.00	209.75	2761.00	22328	0
1956	86.8	1170.00	226.24	2978.00	23018	0
1957	92.8	1223.00	243.94	3211.00	23771	0
1958	109.9	1492.00	272.73	3590.00	26600	0
1959	124.1	1615.00	315.12	4148.00	26173	0
1960	121.6	1591.00	353.18	4649.00	25880	0
1961	83.9	1119.00	368.00	4844.00	25590	0
1962	79.1	1046.00	375.52	4943.00	25910	0
1963	89.4	1158.00	389.42	5126.00	26640	0
1964	101	1349.00	409.40	5389.00	27736	0
1965	113	1578.00	437.13	5754.00	28670	0
1966	131.7	1846.00	472.84	6224.00	29805	0
1967	121.2	1713.00	495.93	6528.00	30814	0
1968	117.5	1601.00	518.57	6826.00	31915	0
1969	133.9	1910.00	545.69	7183.00	33225	0
1970	169.1	2355.00	592.64	7801.00	34432	0
1971	179.5	2520.00	644.61	8485.00	35620	0
1972	183.6	2592.00	693.83	9133.00	35854	0
1973	201.1	2807.00	750.13	9874.00	36652	0
1974	204.1	2839.00	806.42	10615.00	37369	0
1975	221.9	3075.00	869.48	11445.00	38168	0
1976	220.2	2993.00	926.30	12193.00	38834	0
1977	231.3	3227.00	989.51	13025.00	39377	0
1978	263.8	3624.00	1056.80	14112.00	40152	0
1979	286.1	3900.00	1122.00	15273.00	41024	1
1980	302.9	4204.00	1196.24	16438.00	42361	2
1981	313.3	4425.00	1268.02	17268.00	43725	3

(*Continued*)

Table 4.4. (*Continued*)

Year	GDP (at 1952 prices)	GDP (at 1978 prices)	K (at 1952 prices)	K (at 1978 prices)	L	t
1982	341.7	4824.00	1353.55	18297.00	45295	4
1983	378.9	5349.00	1455.62	19515.00	46436	5
1984	436.4	6161.00	1573.31	20928.00	48197	6
1985	495.2	6991.00	1725.20	22755.00	49873	7
1986	539	7611.00	1896.34	24822.00	51282	8
1987	601.4	8491.00	2086.90	27123.00	52783	9
1988	669.2	9448.00	2331.22	30085.00	54334	10
1989	696.4	9832.00	2609.71	33445.00	55329	11
1990	723.1	10209.00	2870.25	36565.00	64749	12
1991	789.6	11148.00	3138.07	39776.00	65491	13
1992	902	12735.00	3452.19	43589.00	66152	14
1993	1027.8	14453.00	3887.57	48994.00	66808	15
1994	1162.3	16283.00	4368.90	55006.00	67455	16
1995	1289.3	17994.00	4916.55	61856.00	68065	17
1996	1418.5	19719.00	5509.09	69304.00	68950	18
1997	1550.1	21455.00	6117.36	77218.00	69820	19
1998	1671.6	23129.00	6752.19	85692.00	70637	20
1999	1799.1		7423.75		71394	21
2000	1950.6		8095.97		72085	22
2001	2112.5		8828.28		73025	23
2002	2304.5		9643.65		73740	24
2003	2535.6		10605.83		74432	25.
2004	2791.2		11675.23		75200	26
2005	3076.9		12836.47		75825	27
2006			14127.17		76400	28

out whether such rapid increase in pollution after 2002 is consistent with Equation (4.25). Our regression leads to the following result.

$$\log(e_t) = 2.4553(0.3414) + 1.2448(0.0441)\log(Y_t) \quad R^2 = 0.9900;$$

$$s = 0.0385 \qquad (4.26)$$

Standard errors are given in parentheses, and s denotes the standard error of the regression. Utilizing the relation

$$\log(e) = \gamma^{-1} \log(\delta/\gamma\theta) + \gamma^{-1} \log(Y), \qquad (4.25)$$

an estimate of the coefficient of $\log(Y)$ in (4.26) is 1.2448, giving an estimate of $\gamma = 1/1.2448 = 0.8034$. Using the estimate of the intercept of (4.25) given in (4.26) we have

$$\log(\delta/\theta\gamma) = 2.4553 \times 0.8034 = 1.9726;$$

$$\delta/\theta\gamma = 7.1893 \quad \text{or} \quad \delta/\theta = 5.7759.$$

We will first estimate δ and use the above result to estimate θ. To estimate the parameters of the Cobb–Douglas production function including δ, we do not have data on pollution e before 1997. Even if we did, we could not simply regress $\log Y$ on t, $\log K$, $\log L$ and $\log e$ not only because of multicolinearity of the explanatory variables but because only K and L are considered real inputs, with pollution e being a byproduct. To measure the effect of allowing more pollution on output, given the amounts of K and L, I first regress $\log Y$ on t, $\log K$ and $\log L$. I then subtract this regression to form a new dependent variable for regression on $\log e$. This method of estimation is questionable and is used for illustrating the method of analysis proposed.

The regression of $\log Y$ on t, $\log K$ and $\log L$ using annual observations from 1952 to 2006, excluding the abnormal years 1958–1969 in the periods of the Great Leap Forward and the Cultural Revolution, and with a linear trend t that starts in 1979 $= 1$, is

$$\log Y = -1.9083(1.0195) + 0.6447(0.0542)\log K$$

$$+ 0.2806(0.1287)\log L + 0.0263(0.0027)t;$$

$$R^2 = 0.9983; \quad s = 0.0512.$$

Subtracting the above linear regression (without the intercept) from $\log Y$ to form a new dependent variable $\log Y_{\text{net}}$ and regressing it on $\log e$ gives

$$\log Y_{\text{net}} = -2.7476(0.5040) + 0.06843(0.0417)\log e;$$

$$R^2 = 0.2518; \quad s = 0.04551.$$

This yields an estimate of 0.06843 for δ. Given $\delta/\theta = 5.7759$ we have

$$\theta = 0.06843/5.7759 = 0.01185.$$

The estimates of θ and γ can be used with the data for $e = 113{,}375$ in 1997 to provide an estimate of the cost of pollution as the second term in our utility function.

$$\theta e^{\gamma} = 0.01185(113{,}375)^{0.80334} = 136.21 \qquad (4.27)$$

as compared with real GDP $= 1550.1$ (indexed in 1952 prices). The cost amounts to 8.79% of real GDP.

The above estimates are based on the assumption that an all-knowing and powerful central planner, or an efficient market, is directing China's macroeconomy. If there are market failures our estimate of "green" GDP will be changed. To find a revised estimate of "green" GDP that allows for market failure we first provide in Section 4.7, a market solution to the macroeconomic model of this section and then introduce market failure in Section 4.8 by assuming that natural resources are underpriced. The estimate of "green" GDP will be revised accordingly.

4.7. Market Solution for the Model of Section 4.5 and the Pricing of Air Pollution Permits

In this section, we provide a market solution to the optimization problem of the previous section and suggest how the implicit price of air pollution permits can be used as a guide to regulate China's air pollution. As in Section 4.4, we take the behavior of the consumer and of the producer in turn.

The representative consumer maximizes

$$\begin{aligned}
L = \Sigma\{&\beta^t[\log(C_t - \theta E_{t+1}^{\gamma})] \\
&- \beta^{t+1}\lambda_{t+1}[K_{t+1} - (1 - d + r_t)K_t + C_t - w_t - q_t e_t] \\
&- \beta^{t+1}\mu_{t+1}[E_{t+1} - b_1 E_t - b_2 e_t]\}, \qquad (4.28)
\end{aligned}$$

with respect to the control variables C_t and e_t and the state variables K_t and E_t.

Differentiating β^{-t} times L with respect to the control variable C_t and the state variable K_t, respectively, and setting the partial derivatives equal to zero yield:

$$(C_t - \theta E_{t+1}^{\gamma})^{-1} - \beta\lambda_{t+1} = 0 \quad \text{or} \quad \beta\lambda_{t+1} = (C_t - \theta E_{t+1}^{\gamma})^{-1},$$
$$(4.29)$$

$$\beta(1 - d + r_t)\lambda_{t+1} - \lambda_t = 0. \tag{4.30}$$

Using (4.29) to substitute for λ_t in (4.30) gives

$$(C_t - \theta E_{t+1}^{\gamma}) = \beta(1 - \delta + r_t)(C_{t-1} - \theta E_t^{\gamma}) \tag{4.31}$$

Differentiating L with respect to e_t yields

$$q_t\lambda_{t+1} + b_2\mu_{t+1} = 0. \tag{4.32}$$

Differentiation with respect to E_t gives

$$-\beta^{-1}\theta\gamma(C_{t-1} - \theta E_t^{\gamma})^{-1}E_t^{\gamma-1} - \mu_t + \beta b_1\mu_{t+1} = 0. \tag{4.33}$$

Using (4.32) to replace μ_t and μ_{t+1} in (4.33) gives

$$-\beta^{-1}\theta\gamma(C_{t-1} - \theta E_t^{\gamma})^{-1}E_t^{\gamma-1} + b_2^{-1}q_{t-1}\lambda_t - \beta b_1 b_2^{-1}q_t\lambda_{t+1} = 0.$$

Using (4.29) to replace λ_t and λ_{t+1} gives

$$-\beta^{-1}\theta\gamma(C_{t-1} - \theta E_t^{\gamma})^{-1}E_t^{\gamma-1} + \beta^{-1}b_2^{-1}q_{t-1}(C_{t-1} - \theta E_t^{\gamma})^{-1}$$
$$- b_1 b_2^{-1}q_t(C_t - \theta E_{t+1}^{\gamma})^{-1} = 0. \tag{4.34}$$

In the special case of $b_1 = 0, b_2 = 1$,

$$q_t = \theta\gamma e_t^{\gamma-1} \quad \text{or} \quad e_t = (q_t/\theta\gamma)^{1-\gamma}, \tag{4.35}$$

which is the supply equation of emission permits e.

The producer's problem is similar to that of Section 4.4. The demand equation for pollution permits is

$$q_t = \delta A_t K_t^{\alpha} L_t^{1-\alpha} e_t^{\delta-1} = \delta Y_t e_t^{-1}. \tag{4.36}$$

Equation (4.36) states that in a competitive market payment to a factor qe equals a fraction δ of output Y. Equating demand and supply gives a result identical to Equation (4.24), which was derived from optimization by a central planner:

$$\delta Y_t = \theta \gamma e_t^{\gamma}.$$

We have estimated in Equation (4.27) that, without market failure, the second term of $Y - \theta e_t^{\gamma}$ in 1997 is $\theta e^{\gamma} = 0.01185(113,375)^{0.80334} = 136.21$ as compared with real GDP of 1550.1 or 8.79%. The payment to pollution is $e_t q_t = \delta Y_t$, where $\delta = 0.068429$. If we raise the price q, the demand $e = \delta Y / q$ would be reduced. In 1997, $e = 113,375$, $Y = 1550.1$ and $\delta Y = 106.07$. This gives the price of the natural resource as $q = \delta Y / e = 0.0009356$.

4.8. Effect of Government or Market Failure on the Behavior of the Macroeconomy

The above econometric analysis using the model of Section 4.5 or 4.7 assumes that the Chinese macroeconomy is controlled by an all-knowing central planner or by a market system with demand and supply working perfectly. If there is government or market failure in the regulation of pollution, how would our model be affected?

Using our model, government failure can be interpreted as the government using a utility function without due consideration of the disutility of pollution. In other words in the utility function

$$\log(Y - \theta e^{\gamma}) = \log(AK^{\alpha}L^{1-\alpha}e^{\delta} - \theta e^{\gamma}),$$

the parameter θ is understated. After the dynamic optimization process is performed to find the relation between pollution and output the same equation

$$\log(e) = \gamma^{-1}\log(\delta/\gamma\theta) + \gamma^{-1}\log(Y) \tag{4.25}$$

would result except that the value of the parameter θ is smaller. Similarly, market failure can be interpreted as the representative consumer using a utility function with an understated θ. This would not affect the form of his supply equation for emission permits

$$e_t = (q_t/\theta\gamma)^{1-\gamma} \tag{4.35}$$

but would only shift the supply curve to the right because of the smaller value of θ used. Hence all our theoretical analysis and statistical estimation procdure for the model of Section 4.5 or 4.7 remain valid.

When the value of θ is smaller, the intercept in Equation (4.25) explaining $\log(e)$ by $\log(Y)$ will increase, leading to more pollution for a given quantity of output. Similarly, the estimate of green GDP as $(Y - \theta e^\gamma)$ would also be affected. Less would be subtracted from GDP on account of environmental damage.

The model of Section 4.6 explains the empirical relation between pollution and GDP extremely well. The model is constructed under the presupposition that there is an economic planner maximizing a multi-period objective function for China. Equivalently, there is a market of emission permits where the producers use environmental capital by purchasing emission permits and the government controls the amount of pollution allowed, or limits the number of permits issued and charges the producers for polluting. Government or market failure in this model can be interpreted as the government or the representative consumer with property rights of environmental capital using a utility function that gives less weight to the pollution term in the utility function. All the analysis based on this model remains valid.

Let me try to use this model to explain the increase in air pollution in China in relation to the increase in GDP for the few years up to 2006. On the demand side, there was a rapid increase in national output and construction activities associated with what the Chinese government officials called an overheating of the macroeconomy. The overheating, if the term is used, came from two sources. One was an unanticipated increase in money supply associated with a rapid inflow of foreign exchange that was converted into RMB. The trade surplus of China was partly due to an undervaluation of the exchange rate of the Chinese currency. According to a well-known and well-documented proposition of Milton Friedman, such an unanticipated increase in money supply would lead to an almost immediate increase in national output and also to increases in prices with delays. This proposition was again confirmed by the data on the Chinese macroeconomy as documented in Chow and Shen (2005). The second was a large increase in construction activities that can be explained by local government officials who could benefit by approving publicly owned land under their control for urban development during their term of office. This phenomenon can be interpreted as an increase in supply where government officials as suppliers of natural resources shifted the supply curve to the right by lower the price of a given quantity supplied. Hence, we have observed that as GDP increased in recent years in China pollution also increased.

References

Chow, Gregory C. (2015). Chapter 5, *China's Economic Transformation*, 3rd edn., UK: Wiley. Forthcoming.

Chow, Gregory C. and Y. K. Kwan (1996). "Economic Effects of Political Movements in China: Lower Bound Estimates," *Pacific Economic Review*, 1(1), 13–26.

Chow, Gregory C. and Yan Shen (2005). "Money, Price Level and Output in the Chinese Macro-economy," *Asia-Pacific Journal of Accounting and Economics*, 12(2), 91–111.

Kwan, Y. K. and Gregory C. Chow (1996). "Estimating Economic Effects of Political Movements in China," *Journal of Comparative Economics*, 23, 192–208.

Shi, Minjun and Ma, Guoxla (2009). *Real Price of China's Economic Growth: An Empirical Study of Genuine Savings* (in Chinese), Science Press.

Xerapadeas, A. (2005). "Economic Growth and the Environment," in Maler K, Vincent J, (ed) *Handbook of Environmental Economics*, vol 3. North–Holland, Amsterdam.

Questions

1. Introduce cumulative pollution into the first model of this chapter by setting up the Lagrangean

$$
\begin{aligned}
L = \sum_t \{ & \beta^t [\log C_t + \theta \log(M - E_{t+1})] \\
& - \beta^{t+1} \lambda_{t+1} [K_{t+1} - (1-d)K_t - aK_t + C_t] \\
& - \beta^{t+1} \mu_{t+1} [E_{t+1} - b_1 E_t - b_2 ca K_t] \}
\end{aligned}
\tag{2}
$$

where output $Y = aK$, emission $e_t = caK_t$ and cumulated emission E_{t+1} is subject to the dynamic constraint multiplied by μ_{t+1}. The central planer maximizes L with respect to the control variable C and state variables K and E.

2. Provide a market solution to the model of question 1.

3. Introduce scrubbing into the model of Section 4.2 by assuming that pollution can be reduced by using a technology of scrubbing. Let s be the amount of pollution to be scrubbed away and s be treated as a control variable.

Chapter 5

Stochastic Models to Study the Effect of Climate Change

5.1. Introduction

Stochastic models are now introduced to study the effect of climate change and the policies to deal with it. The parameters of the models are assumed to be known in this chapter but possibly unknown in Chapter 6. In Section 5.2, I first use a simple model of economic growth for deciding whether to mitigate the harmful effect of climate change in the future by using resources at present. A main purpose of this exercise is to explain a method for studying this important question. In Section 5.3, I will study the uncertain effect of global warming on economic growth through its effect on aggregate investment in a macroeconomic model by way of its effect on expected future profits. The methodology used is similar to that of Nordhaus (2008) and Nordhaus and Boyer (2000) in using a stochastic model to evaluate different policies, although our model is much simpler and the policies are more limited in scope. Section 5.4 discusses the effect of introducing uncertainty in the parameters of a macroeconomic model on the solution for optimum behavior.

5.2. A Simple Macroeconomic Model for Deciding Whether to Mitigate the Effect of Climate Change: An Exposition of the Lagrange Method for Stochastic Control

The effects of possible future damages due to climate change and of the discount rate on the decision whether to devote resources to prevent global warming can also be demonstrated by using the well-known Brock–Mirman model of economic growth as presented in

Chow (1997, Section 3.1). In this discussion, I assume the stochastic model describing the economy to be known. The damage of climate change to the economy in a given future year T is also known, and specified to be 1-b of world output in that date, leaving only a fraction b of output produced for consumption. Using the Brock–Mirman model, we will discuss how to choose between two alternatives. The first alternative is not to mitigate the effect of climate change and to allow the damage in the given future year to take place. Under this alternative, in year T, global warming will reduce world output to a given fraction b. The second alternative is to prevent the harmful effect of global warming to take place in year T by sacrificing a given percent of consumption each year.

For this economy, we assume that a central planner maximizes the following objective function

$$\text{Max}_c \boldsymbol{E}_1 \sum_{t=1}^{T} \beta^t \log c_t, \tag{5.1}$$

subject to

$$k_{t+1} = k_t^\alpha z_t - c_t \tag{5.2}$$

Here c denotes consumption per worker-consumer, $k^\alpha z$ denotes the amount of output (to be used as capital good or consumption good in this one-good economy) produced per worker-consumer where z is a random shock to total factor productivity, with $\log z_t$ assumed to be independently distributed with mean zero. The expectation sign E_1 denotes mathematical expectation conditioned on information available at the beginning of period 1. This model will be used to calculate the expected total utility under two policy options. The first is not to devote resources to mitigate the harmful effect of global warming and allow it to take place at a given future period T. The second is to sacrifice a given fraction of consumption each year until year T, which is assumed to prevent or reduce the harmful effect of global warming in year T.

In order to calculate expected utilities under two specified policy options, it is necessary to solve the social planner's dynamic optimization problem. Again, I will use the Lagrange method by introducing the Lagrangean

$$L = E_1 \sum_{t=1}^{T} \{\beta^t \log c_t - \beta^{t+1}\lambda_{t+1}(k_{t+1} - k_t^\alpha z_t + c_t)\} \qquad (5.3)$$

and set its partial derivatives with respect to the control variable c_t and the state variable k_t equal to zero, yielding

$$c_t^{-1} = \beta E_t \lambda_{t+1}, \qquad (5.4)$$

$$\lambda_t = \beta \alpha \, k_t^{\alpha-1} z_t \, E_t \lambda_{t+1}. \qquad (5.5)$$

When the model is stochastic, the objective function and the Lagrangean are both mathematical expectations. To maximize the Lagrangean, we simply differentiate the expressions on the right-hand-side of the expectation sign. Since a mathematical expectation is an integral, this operation amounts to differentiating first before evaluating the integral, a procedure that is valid under fairly general mathematical conditions. After we take the derivatives of the terms in curly brackets on the right-hand-side of (5.3), we take expectations to obtain the first-order conditions (5.4) and (5.5). Note that we have changed the expectation sign before the derivatives with respect to c_t and k_t from E_1 to E_t. This is justified because at time t when the decision on c_t is chosen, the information at time t is available and we can take expectation E_t given the information available at the beginning of period t.

As in the case of optimal control for deterministic models, the first-order conditions (5.4) and (5.5) are two functional equations. They can be used to solve for the control variable c_t and the Lagrange multiplier λ_t as functions of the state variables k_t and z_t. Note that z_t is also a state variable in this problem because the optimum value of the control variable depends on its value, but it is assumed to be distributed independently through time and thus does not require a dynamic constraint as in the case of the state variable k. Hence there is no Lagrange multiplier associated with its evolution through time and no need to differentiate z_t to obtain the optimum solution.

Because of the particular functional forms chosen for the objective function and the dynamic constraint in this model, the solution of the functional equations for c_t and λ_t takes explicit forms. If the time horizon T is infinity (not true for our problem), these functions are time-invariant. A common procedure used to solve for such explicit functions is to make an educated guess (an art perfected by experience) of the functional form for c_t or λ_t and substitute the function in the first-order conditions. The first-order conditions then become algebraic equations that can be used to solve for the unknown parameters of the functions for c_t and λ_t. This is exactly the same procedure employed in the case of a linear dynamic equation and a quadratic objective function when we propose a linear function for the vector multiplier $\lambda = Hx + h$. For the infinite horizon case, we propose the function $c_t = dk_t^\alpha z_t$, with the parameter d yet to be determined. In this case, the first-order conditions (5.4) and (5.5) are functional equations that are valid for all periods t. Hence the optimal feedback control function $c_t = dk_t^\alpha z_t$ is also valid for all periods.

By using (5.4) to replace $E_t\lambda_{t+1}$ in (5.5) and substituting this proposed function for c_t we obtain $\lambda_t = d^{-1}\alpha k_t^{-1}$. Using this function for λ_t we evaluate

$$\lambda_{t+1} = d^{-1}\alpha k_{t+1}^{-1} = d^{-1}\alpha(k_t^\alpha z_t - dk_t^\alpha z_t)^{-1}.$$

Substituting these two functions for λ_t and λ_{t+1}, respectively, in Equation (5.5) and noting $E_t(k_t^\alpha z_t - dk_t^\alpha z_t)^{-1} = (k_t^\alpha z_t - dk_t^\alpha z_t)^{-1}$ since z_t is given information at time t, we equate coefficients on both sides of the resulting equation to obtain $d = 1 - \beta\alpha$. Thus the optimum consumption function for the infinite horizon case is

$$c_t = (1 - \beta\alpha)k_t^\alpha z_t \tag{5.6}$$

and the solution for λ_t is

$$\lambda_t = d^{-1}\alpha k_t^{-1} = (1 - \beta\alpha)^{-1}\alpha k_t^{-1}. \tag{5.7}$$

Given the consumption function (5.6), we can find an equation for the evolution of k_t:

$$k_{t+1} = k_t^\alpha z_t - c_t = \beta\alpha k_t^\alpha z_t, \tag{5.8}$$

implying

$$\log k_{t+1} = \log(\beta\alpha) + \alpha \log k_t + \log z_t. \qquad (5.9)$$

Thus under optimal control, $\log k_t$ is a first-order autoregression with coefficient α and intercept $\log(\beta\alpha)$.

To deal with the problem of global warming we will study the dynamic optimization problem for a finite time horizon T. First consider the special case of two time periods, or $T = 2$. The Lagrangean (after divided by β) is

$$L = E_1\{\log c_1 + \beta \log c_2 - \beta\lambda_2(k_2 - k_1^{\alpha}z_1 + c_1)\}. \qquad (5.10)$$

If we ignore the question on whether to devote resources to mitigate the harmful effect of climate change, the problem is to choose the consumption c_1 and c_2 for the two periods to maximize this Lagrangean. Since the world ends in period 2, the amount of good k_2 available in period 2 should be devoted entirely for consumption, i.e., $k_2 = c_2$. The constraint in this problem is $c_1 + c_2 = k_1^{\alpha}z_1$. In other words, the output $k_1^{\alpha}z_1$ in period 1 can be used for consumption in period 1 or period 2. Differentiating L with respect to c_1 and c_2 gives

$$c_1^{-1} = \beta E \lambda_2,$$
$$\beta c_2^{-1} = \beta E \lambda_2,$$

implying

$$c_2 = \beta c_1.$$

Using the total output constraint, we have $c_1 + \beta c_1 = k_1^{\alpha}z_1$ or $c_1 = (1 + \beta)^{-1}k_1^{\alpha}z_1$. Thus, the dynamic optimization problem is solved.

To deal with the problem of global warming, I consider two options when consumption in period 2 could be damaged by global warming. If no resource is devoted in period 1 to mitigate the harmful effect of global warming, consumption in period 2 will equal only to a fraction b of the output. Let us assume that if 3% of output in period 1 is devoted to mitigate the effect of global warming all output available in period 2 can be consumed.

Under option 1, the optimization problem is specified by the Lagrangean

$$L_1 = E_1\{\log c_1 + \beta \log c_2 - \beta \lambda_2 (c_2/b - k_1^\alpha z_1 + c_1)\}. \tag{5.11}$$

Output for period 2 needs to be c_2/b in order that a fraction b of it will be available for consumption in period 2. The first-order conditions are $c_1^{-1} = \beta \lambda_2$ and $\beta c_2^{-1} = \beta \lambda_2/b$, implying $c_2 = b\beta c_1$. The budget constraint becomes $c_1 + \beta c_1 = k_1^\alpha z_1$, implying

$$c_1 = (1 + \beta)^{-1} k_1^\alpha z_1 \quad \text{and} \quad c_2 = b\beta(1 + \beta)^{-1} k_1^\alpha z_1. \tag{5.12}$$

Under option 2, the optimization problem is specified by the Lagrangean

$$L_2 = E_1\{\log c_1 + \beta \log c_2 - \beta \lambda_2 (c_2 - 0.97\, k_1^\alpha z_1 + c_1)\}. \tag{5.13}$$

The first-order conditions are $c_1^{-1} = \beta \lambda_2$ and $\beta c_2^{-1} = \beta \lambda_2$, implying $c_2 = \beta c_1$. The solution is $c_1 + \beta c_1 = 0.97\, k_1^\alpha z_1$ or

$$c_1 = 0.97(1 + \beta)^{-1} k_1^\alpha z_1 \quad \text{and} \quad c_2 = 0.97\beta(1 + \beta)^{-1} k_1^\alpha z_1. \tag{5.14}$$

The two-period utility $\log c_1 + \beta \log c_2$ for the two options would be equal if and only if (seen more easily by the normalization $k_1^\alpha z_1 = 1$)

$$-\log(1 + \beta) + \beta[\log b + \log \beta - \log(1 + \beta)]$$
$$= \log(0.97) - \log(1 + \beta) + \beta[\log(0.97) + \log \beta - \log(1 + \beta)]$$

or

$$\beta \log b = (1 + \beta) \log(0.97). \tag{5.15}$$

If the left-hand-side is larger than the right-hand-side, option 1 will be chosen. Otherwise, option 2 will be chosen or resource will be spent to mitigate global warming. See question 1 for an exercise to set up the calculation for determining the two options.

5.3. Modeling the Uncertain Effect of Global Warming on Investment in the World Economy

In our macromodeling of the effect of pollution or emission of pollutants in Chapter 4, deterministic models were used. One way to introduce the effect of global warming in a stochastic model of the world is to allow the expectation of the adverse effect of global warming in the future to influence investment decision and thus the course of economic development.

In our deterministic models of Chapter 4, investment decision of the firm plays a passive role. The representative consumer is assumed to maximize a multiperiod utility function subject to a budget constraint for every period, and investment or capital accumulation is determined by this maximization process. The representative firm simply maximizes profit in each period. In order to allow for the effect on global warming on the evolution of the world economy I propose to take two steps. First, the model of Chapter 4 needs to be changed to make investment decision dependent on the firm maximizing expected sum of discounted net revenues minus expenditures on investment in the future. Second, expected net revenues in the future will be assumed to depend on the possible adverse effects of global warming on the world economy. We will follow these two steps below. The basic idea can be found in Nordhaus and Boyer (2000) although we do not use their model, which is fairly complicated. That model is one version of the DICE model, an acronym for Dynamic Integrated model of Climate and the Economy.

In our model to study the effect of expectations of damage from global warming on investment, let us first study the investment behavior of the firm. The consumer is assumed to be passive as far as investment is concerned since he/she only receives income from dividends that enters the budget constraint. We assume the consumer to maximize the sum of expected discounted utilities of consumption C_t subject to the dynamic constraint on the accumulation of wealth W_t

$$W_{t+1} = W_t + w_t L_t + r_t K_t + D_t - C_t.$$

Here, there are three sources of income: labor income, which is the product of wage rate w and quantity of labor L supplied, which we assume to be fixed as in Chapter 4, capital income and dividend D_t which the firm owned by the consumer distributes during year t. The Lagrangean representing this maximization problem is

$$L = \Sigma\{\beta^t \log C_t + \beta^{t+1}\lambda_{t+1}[W_{t+1} - W_t - w_t L_t - r_t K_t - D_t + C_t]\}$$

$$(5.17)$$

The control variable is C_t and the state variable is W_t. L_t is fixed and D_t is dividend received passively from the firm owned by the consumer. Differentiating (5.17) with respect to C_t and W_t gives two first-order conditions to determine C_t and W_t.

The representative firm is assumed to maximize the expected sum of discounted future net income, which equals profit Π minus investment I financed only through its own saving. The Lagrangean for this maximization problem is

$$L = \Sigma\{\beta^t[A_t K_t^\alpha L_t^{1-\alpha} - r_t K_t - w_t L_t - D_t - I_t]$$

$$- \beta^{t+1}\mu_{t+1}[K_{t+1} - (1-d)K_t - I_t]\}. \qquad (5.18)$$

The control variables are L_t (to determine the demand for labor and the wage rate even when the supply of labor L_t by the consumer is assumed to be fixed), D_t and I_t. The state variable is K_t. Differentiating (5.18) with respect to the three control variables and the state variable gives four first order conditions to determine L_t, D_t, I_t and K_t.

Solving the consumer's maximization problem gives two first-order conditions, and solving the firm's maximization problem gives four first order conditions. These six first-order conditions (including the two first-order conditions from solving the consumer's problem) determine the evolution of the six variables C_t, W_t, L_t, D_t, I_t and K_t. (Given the demand for L_t and K_t, the wage rate w_t and the interest rate r_t will be determined.) Note that the first-order conditions obtained by differentiation with respect to the state variables W and K determine the Lagrange multipliers as functions of the state variables. The two dynamic equations determine the values of the two state variables for the next period, which are used as data in the optimization problem for the next period. In this way, investment behavior can be modeled for studying the possible effects of global warming.

As a second part of this modeling effort, we need to allow the expectation of future profits to affect investment that the above model has ignored. To do so, we treat productivity A_t as a random variable and add the expectation sign E_1 on the left of the summation sign in the Lagrangean for the firm (5.18) as we did in expression (5.3). To illustrate how this model can be used to evaluate a policy to reduce emission or pollution, assume that if we use a fraction α of output to reduce emission, utility will be increased by an amount $\theta \log(1 + \alpha)$. In the new model, A_t will be replaced by $(1 - \alpha)A_t$ and a term $\theta \log(1 + \alpha)$ will be added to the utility function. Comparing the solution of this new model with the solution of the original model will enable us to evaluate the above policy to reduce pollution. Other parametric changes can be made to incorporate the effects of policies to reduce emission on the performance of a macro-economy. We have just outlined a method to incorporate investment in models to determine optimal policies for controlling climate change. A pioneering effort in this direction can be found in Nordhaus and Boyer (2000).

What can be accomplished by having such a macroeconomic model? Economic models are constructed to explain the evolution of an economy or parts of an economy and possibly to forecast future development of an economy. In the present case, explaining past behavior is not the main purpose. As far as forecasting is concerned, since the assumed effect of global warming on investment behavior is based on limited knowledge, the model cannot be relied upon to produce accurate forecasts. The modeling exercise of this section thus has a similar objective as the calculations presented in Section 5.2, namely to give warning signals to policy makers on what the future development of the macro-economy may be if we do not pay attention to prevent the possibly damaging effects of global warming from occurring.

5.4. A Macroeconomic Model Incorporating an Uncertain Effect of Pollution

Let us begin with the following macromodel. The government is supposed to be a central planner who solves a dynamic optimization problem to guide the economy that is represented by the following Lagrangean expression

$$L = \sum_t \{\beta^t [\log C_t + \theta \log(M - E_t)$$
$$- \beta^{t+1} \lambda_{t+1} [K_{t+1} - (1 - d)K_t - Y_t + C_t]$$
$$- \beta^{t+1} \mu_{t+1} [E_{t+1} - b_1 E_t - b_2 e_t]\} \tag{5.19}$$

The definitions of all variables are the same as those used in Section 4.5. Uncertainty can be introduced into this model by making the parameter $\theta = \theta_t$ stochastic or by adding a random disturbance in the dynamic equation explaining E_{t+1}. An expectation sign E_1 will be added before the summation sign in the Lagrangean (5.19). See Chow (1997, Chapter 2) for an exposition of the Lagrange method for dynamic optimization using stochastic models in discrete time which is more general than the exposition given in Section 5.2.

If a random disturbance enters additively in the dynamic equation determining the state variable E_{t+1}, the solution for the optimal control equations will not be affected as the reader can easily check because the model is linear. Furthermore, and perhaps more importantly, the equation explaining E_{t+1} is quite accurate and the value of any random disturbance added will be very small and negligible.

A more important problem of uncertainly is concerned with the second term in the utility function. If the effect of the pollution variable $(M - E_t)$ is uncertain, θ in the second term of the utility function should be replaced by a random variable θ_t. (In applications where a Cobb-Douglas production is used to measure "green GDP" $Y_t = A_t K_t^\alpha L_t^{1-\alpha} e_t^\delta$, this term can be interpreted as the logarithm of total factor productivity A_t in the production function with $A_t = (M - E_t)^\theta$, but we do not use this interpretation here.)

The Lagrangean for this optimum stochastic control problem becomes

$$L = \sum_t E_t \{ \beta^t [\log C_t + \theta_t \log(M - E_t)$$
$$- \beta^{t+1} \lambda_{t+1} [K_{t+1} - (1 - d)K_t - Y_t + C_t]$$
$$- \beta^{t+1} \mu_{t+1} [E_{t+1} - b_1 E_t - b_2 e_t] \}. \tag{5.20}$$

The derivation of the optimal solution here follows closely the derivation in Section 4.5. Differentiation of L with respect to C_t and K_t recalling $Y_t = A_t K_t^\alpha L_t^{1-\alpha} e_t^\delta$, yields similar first-order conditions as before, now recorded below for convenience.

$$C_t^{-1} = \beta E_t \lambda_{t+1}, \tag{5.21}$$

$$\lambda_t = \beta[1 - d + \alpha Y_t K_t^{-1}] E_t \lambda_{t+1}. \tag{5.22}$$

Differentiation of L with respect to e_t and E_t, respectively, yields

$$\delta Y_t e_t^{-1} E_t \lambda_{t+1} = -b_2 E_t \mu_{t+1}, \tag{5.23}$$

$$\mu_t = -(E_t \theta_t)(M - E_t)^{-1} + \beta b_1 E_t \mu_{t+1}. \tag{5.24}$$

Here we assume that the uncertainty on θ_t is not resolved at the beginning of time t. Using (5.23) to substitute for the μ's in (5.24) and then using (5.21) to substitute for the λ's give

$$b_2^{-1} \beta^{-1} \delta Y_t e_t^{-1} C_t^{-1} = (E_t \theta_{t+1})(M - b_1 E_t - b_2 e_t)^{-1}$$
$$+ b_1 b_2^{-1} \delta E_t Y_{t+1} e_{t+1}^{-1} C_{t+1}^{-1}. \tag{5.25}$$

In the special case when $b_1 = 0$ and $b_2 = 1$, Equation (5.25) implies

$$\beta^{-1} \delta Y_t e_t^{-1} C_t^{-1} = (E_t \theta)(M - b_1 E_t - b_2 e_t)^{-1}, \tag{5.26}$$

where we make use of $E_t \theta_{t+1} = E_t \theta_t \equiv E_t \theta$. If we compare this derivation of the first-order conditions with the one that we can derive from a similar model with a non-stochastic θ, we find that the two are identical except for the substitution of $E\theta$ in this derivation for θ in the model with certainty. In stochastic control problems, if we replace a stochastic variable in the solution by its mathematical expectation, the solution is known as a "certainty equivalent" solution. In general, a "certainty equivalent solution" will not be the same as the truly optimum solution but may be a close approximation. In this example, the "certainty equivalent" solution is the same as the optimum solution derived by the first-order conditions.

We have thus found that for the model above, introducing uncertainty by making the parameter θ in the second term of the utility function (for measuring the negative effect of damage to the environment) stochastic will not change the nature of the optimum solution to the problem, except for substituting θ_t by its mathematical expectation. This simple substitution is possible because the random variable enters linearly in the utility function. The certainty equivalence solution is also optimum if a stochastic disturbance enters additively in the equation determining the evolution of E_t.

If the distribution of the effect of global warming θ_t has a long tail to the right the probability for a very low utility represented by the term $\theta_t \log(M - E_t)$ for $(M - E_t)$ near zero to occur is substantial. The economy is subject to a great deal of risk in period t. The optimum action remains to be the certainty equivalent solution. Thus the risk of having a very small utility due to a long tail in the distribution of θ_t is reflected only by the mean of its distribution. This statement does not affect our previous analysis of the issue on whether to worry about global warming because we are now choosing an optimal policy given a stochastic model and not deciding on the urgency of the global warming issue.

5.5.   Different Purposes of an Optimization Model

There are several purposes that an economic model can serve as demonstrated by the models presented in this book.

1. An economic model can be used as a logical exercise to make a meaningful economic proposition. The opening page of the classic treatise of Samuelson (1947) contains a statement, "Mathematics is a language". A logical statement put in the form of mathematics makes it precise and clear. Mathematics is used to deduce

propositions from assumptions. We gave an example of this use in Section 1.2 on a simple model of pollution. We expressed the utility function as

$$\log c + \theta \log(M - e)$$

and showed that the optimum amount of pollution is $e = M\delta/(\theta + \delta)$, which is a meaningful economic proposition expressed precisely and concisely.

2. Related to the first, a model as a mathematical exercise helps us think clearly about a problem. When the optimum amount of pollution is expressed above, we know what parameters or factors affect it and in what way.

3. When a model describes different sectors of an economy, it can be used to describe the behavior of economic agents in each sector and the conditions of equilibrium. A simplest example is given in Section 1.3, where the behavior of consumers and of firms are captured, and the equilibrium shows that the market solution to the amount of pollution equals to the amount determined by a central economic planner. The result provides a proof for a special case of the working of the "invisible hand" of Adam Smith.

4. A model can be made quantitative if it is expressed as an econometric model and its parameters are estimated by econometric methods. Such a model can be used to explain economic data.

5. An econometric model can also be used to forecast economic variables.

6. An econometric model can be used to suggest suitable policies for action.

The model of Section 5.2 is logical exercise used to answer the question whether we should worry about global warming today. The model of Section 5.3 is used to answer the same question. In principle, it can be estimated econometrically using the techniques presented in Chapter 4, but it is not useful for making econometric forecasts because the assumed effects of expectation of future damage from global warming on current investment are only good enough as a logical exercise to answer the above question but not quantitatively accurate enough to make econometric forecasts for the future.

The model of Section 5.4 is small and manageable. It can be estimated econometrically as the models in Chapter 4 and be used for forecasting and providing an optimum time path for CO_2 emission to solve the global warming problem, and not just to decide whether to worry about this problem. Using this model, we can determine the highest value of the objective function associated with the optimum solution. If this value is low, that means under the present economic and technical conditions, global warming is a serious problem and we probably should denote more resources, perhaps in R&D, to slow down global warming. This is one way to answer the question whether we should worry about global warming today. If the value of the objective function generated by the optimum path is high enough, we do not have to worry; otherwise there is cause for worry. An advantage of constructing models of this kind is that it not only provides an answer to the question whether we should worry about the problem of global warming but also tells us how best to control CO_2 emission. The models of the type presented in Sections 5.2 and 5.3 cannot be used in this way.

In the model of Section 5.4, the problem of whether to worry about global warming is not taken into consideration when we perform the dynamic optimization exercise to find the optimal path for CO_2 emission. However, such a model may be realistic enough to give us a warning that the expected value of the objective function associated with the optimal path is so low that we have to worry about the problem of global warming today, in the sense that we need find ways to reduce the rate of CO_2 emission today. All models introduced in this book up to this point fail to incorporate the possible effects of technological innovations. Economic models can be used to make long-term forecasts if there is technological change by assuming certain kinds of technological change to be given. The most common example is an exponential trend in total factor productivity in an aggregate production function. For studying the problems of the environment, however, technological change may be expected to take place as discrete historical events that change the way energy is produced. Second, as will be pointed out in Section 6.4 when discussing the work of Weitzman (2009), models cannot be estimated with known accuracy if the information used is not data generated by random samples. This is a limitation of econometric models and not of simulation models.

References

Chow, Gregory C. (1997). *Dynamic Economics: Optimization by the Lagrange Method*. New York: Oxford University Press.

Nordhaus, W. D. (2008). *A Question of Balance: Weighing the Options on Global Warming Policies*. Yale University Press.

Nordhaus, William D. and Joseph Boyer (2000). *Warming the World: Economic Models of Global Warming*. Cambridge, MA: MIT Press.

Samuelson, Paul (1947). *Foundations of Economic Analysis*. Cambridge: Harvard University Press.

Weitzman, Martin L. (2009). "On Modeling and Improving the Economics of Catastrophic Climate Change." *Review of Economics and Statistics*, 91, 1–19.

Questions

1. Set up the problem of choosing between the two options when faced with the possible damage of global warming as presented in Section 5.2 for the case $T = 3$. Write down the Lagrangean for this problem. State the first-order conditions for optimum and the remaining steps necessary to decide on whether to devote resources to mitigate global warming without going through the calculations.

Chapter 6

Parameter Uncertainty in Models of Global Warming

6.1. Introduction

In Chapter 5, uncertainty was introduced in a stochastic model describing the dynamic process for the evolution of the state variable (Equation (5.2) of Section 5.2; Equation (5.19) of Section 5.4) or in a parameter of the utility function (Equation (5.20) of Section 5.4). In this chapter, we introduce additional uncertainty by assuming that the probability distribution of the parameters of the dynamic model may be unknown. A key question is, given such uncertainty in the parameters of our dynamic model, whether we should devote resources at present to mitigate the harmful effect of global warming in the future.

In Section 6.2, I will start with a simple example of two periods and of known parameters in order to point out that the probability distribution of world output subject to possible harmful effect of global warming and the discount rate are two important factors affecting the decision whether to devote resources to mitigate global warming. One ought to mitigate the harmful effect of global warming if the harmful effect is large as represented by its probability distribution and if the harmful effect in the future is considered important, i.e., if the discount factor used to discount future income is large or close to one. (Let the discount factor be β; $\beta = 1/(1 + r)$ where r is the discount rate.)

In Section 6.3, we further discuss the effect of the discount rate in the context of a dynamic model for the evolution of the economy, relaxing the assumption of a world of two periods as in the simplified illustration of Section 6.2. In Section 6.4, we further relax the assumption that the parameters of the probability distribution of world output are known and allow the unknown parameters to be inferred by Bayesian statistical inference, following the work of Weitzman (2009). In Section 6.5 I will conclude with comments on Weitzman's approach.

6.2. Two Factors Affecting the Decision Whether to Mitigate Global Warming

Should we try to mitigate the harmful effect of global warming? The answer depends on the probability distribution of the harmful effect of global warming and on the discount rate as will be explained in this chapter. In Chapter 5, a decision maker was assumed to maximize expected utility. In this section, we try to explain and justify the maximization of expected utility in human behavior.

Let us illustrate the theory of maximization of expected utility by considering the decision on whether to buy insurance to guard against a possible accident that may destroy your car. Assume for illustration that there is a 95% probability of having no accident and a 5% probability of having an accident that will destroy your car that costs $20,000. How much insurance are you willing to pay to insure the car for $20,000 (assuming no deductible amount that you need to pay first before the insurance company compensates you)? One answer is based on calculating the mathematical expectation of the value of your possible loss, which is 0.95 times zero plus 0.05 times $20,000, or $1,000. In other words, the expected value of your loss is $1,000. A person making decision under uncertainty by maximizing mathematical expectation of income or minimizing mathematical expectation of loss will be willing to pay $1,000 to insure his car against complete destruction in the above example.

However, most people do not behave so as to minimize expected loss of income. If the $20,000 is very dear to the person who cannot afford to lose it, he/she may be willing to pay more than $1,000 to insure the car. In this case it means that the utility after paying $1,000 for insurance is larger than the utility of having 95% probability of paying nothing but a 5% probability of losing $20,000 of his/her wealth. Let the person's wealth be $50,000 and let the utility function be $u(\ )$. The above statement means

$$u(50000 - 1000) > 0.95u(50000) + 0.05u(30000).$$

If the person's utility function is the natural log function, he/she will decide to buy insurance in this case because log $(49000) = 10.800$ is larger than $0.95 \log(50000) + 0.05 \log(30000) = 10.279 + 0.515 = 10.794$. The amount of insurance x that he is willing to pay is obtained by solving the equation

$$u(50000 - x) = 0.95u(50000) + 0.05u(30000) = 10.794.$$

Turning to the decision on whether to devote resource to mitigate climate change, let us assume: (1) There are two periods, present and future; resource to mitigate climate change is paid in period 1 and harmful effect of climate change occurs in period 2. (2) World income is 50,000 in each period if resource of x units in period 1 is devoted to mitigate climate change. (3) If no resource is used to mitigate global warming, there is 95% probability for climate change to have no effect on world income in period 2 and there is a 5% probability for world income to be reduced by y units due to climate change.

If resource of x units in period 1 is used to mitigate the effect of climate change, with β being the subjective discount rate, the expected utility is:

$$u(50,000 - x) + \beta u(50,000). \tag{6.1}$$

If no resource is used to mitigate climate change the expected utility is

$$u(50,000) + \beta[0.95u(50,000) + 0.05u(50,000 - y)]. \tag{6.2}$$

The world should mitigate climate change if (6.1) is larger than (6.2). After some algebraic simplification, this means if

$$u(50,000 - x) > u(50,000) + 0.05\beta[u(50,000 - y) - u(50,000)]. \tag{6.3}$$

The inequality (6.3) illustrates three points. First, as the cost x to mitigate climate change increases the utility to mitigate climate change decreases, making it less desirable to mitigate change. Second, as β decreases, the future becomes less important, the right-hand-side of (6.3) increases, making it less desirable to mitigate climate change. Third, the larger the damage y (which has a probability of 0.05 of occurring in this example), the smaller the right-hand-side of (6.3), making it more desirable to mitigate climate change. The third point means that the probability distribution of the damage due to climate change is an important factor affecting the decision on whether to mitigate climate change.

6.3. The Importance of the Discount Rate for Mitigating Climate Change in a Continuous-Time Dynamic Model

In the context of a continuous-time dynamic economic model, replacing a model in discrete time for only two periods, the importance of the discount rate can be illustrated by the following discussion by Eytan Sheshinski (2008) on the *Stern Review*. In this example, uncertainty is allowed to occur only in the terminal year 2200 (beginning from year 2000). Let the utility function of world output y be

$$u(y) = \frac{y^{1-\eta}}{1-\eta}, \quad \eta < 1 \tag{6.4}$$

Assume that in year 2200 there is a 0.05 probability that y will be reduced by 3% and a 0.95 probability that y will be reduced by 34%. Let us find the proportional reduction in y occurring for sure in year 2200 which will give the same expected utility as the above situation under uncertainty. Solving Equation (6.5) below for x, we find $x = 0.329$.

$$u(y(1-x)) = (0.05)u(y(1-0.03)) + (0.95)u(y(1-0.34)) \tag{6.5}$$

The solution $x = 0.329$ is called the "certainty equivalent" reduction of GDP in the year 2200 since it would provide the same expected utility level under uncertainty as given on the right-hand-side of Equation (6.5); $y(1-x)$ is the income that generates the same utility as the expected utility on the right-hand-side of Equation (6.5).

We would like to compare the utility of the policy of using resources every year to mitigate the harmful effect of global warming with the utility of the policy of inaction. To do so, we assume that y grows at 1.3% per year and that the resource required to mitigate global warming is 1%. In the case of devoting resource to mitigate global warming the time path of y beginning with y_0 in year $t = 0$ is $y_0\, e^{.013t}$ (.99). In the case of inaction y will be reduced through time, and at the end of 200 years, y will be reduced by 20%. We convert this 20% to a reduction in the annual growth rate, which equals $[\ln(1) - \ln(0.8)]/200 = 0.001$. This means a reduction of the annual growth rate from 1.3% to 1.2%, yielding a time path of y to be $y_0\, e^{.012t}$. For the two options to have the same utility over the 200-year period, Equation (6.6) below must be satisfied, where ρ is the discount rate.

$$\int_{t_0}^{t_1} e^{-\rho t}[u(y_0 e^{.013t}(.99)) - u(y_0 e^{.012t})]dt = 0 \qquad (6.6)$$

$$t_0 = 2000 \quad t_1 = 2200 \quad y_0 = \text{GNP in } 2000$$

The solution of Equation (6.6) for ρ is $\rho = 0.085$. If $\rho = 0$, there is no discounting of the future or the future matters as much as the present. If $\rho < 0.085$, the future counts more than when $\rho = 0.085$ and resources should be devoted to the mitigation of global warming. Since most economists would use a value of ρ smaller than 0.085, the calculation based on the *Stern Review* favors mitigation. This example illustrates how the question whether to devote resources to mitigate global warming depends on the discount factor. In the next section, we will show that the discount factor may be less important if there is uncertainty in a parameter of a stochastic model describing the damage of CO_2 to the environment. In the example of this section, the distribution of the damage is given and there is no parameter uncertainty.

We will now show that a 1.3% rate of growth as assumed above is optimum for a Ramsey growth model with log utility.

In the Ramsey growth model, a representative economic agent solves the problem:

$$Max \int_0^T e^{-\rho t} u(c(t))dt$$

subject to

$$\dot{k}(t) = f(k(t)) - c(t)$$

To perform this constrained maximization for a dynamic model in continuous time, the Pontryagen maximum principle can be applied. Alternatively we can use the following Lagrange method as described in Chow (1997). By this method, we first define $dk(t)$ as $k(t+dt)-k(t)$ for very small t and rewrite the differential equation as

$$dk(t) = k(t+dt) - k(t) = (f(k(t) - c(t)) \, dt.$$

Using the Lagrange multiplier $\lambda(t+dt)$ for the above differential equation viewed as a constraint, we maximize the Lagrange expression

$$L = \int \{ e^{-\rho t} u(c(t)) dt - e^{-\rho(t+dt)} \lambda(t+dt) [(k(t+dt)$$
$$- k(t) - (f(k(t) - c(t)) \, dt] \},$$

with respect to the control variable $c(t)$ and the state variable $k(t)$ for all t.

Differentiating L with respect to $c(t)$ and reversing the order of differentiation and integration give

$$u'(c(t)) \, dt - e^{-\rho dt} \lambda(t+dt) dt = 0.$$

Since the second term can be written as $(1 - \rho dt)(\lambda(t) + d\lambda) dt$, if we ignore terms of order smaller than dt the above first-order condition becomes

$$u'(c(t)) - \lambda(t) = 0. \tag{6.7}$$

Differentiating L with respect to $k(t)$ gives

$$e^{-\rho dt} \lambda(t+dt)[1 + f'(k)dt] - \lambda(t) = 0,$$
$$(1 - \rho dt)(\lambda(t) + d\lambda)[1 + f'(k)dt] - \lambda(t) = 0,$$
$$[\lambda(t) + d\lambda - \lambda\rho dt][1 + f'(k)dt] - \lambda(t) = 0,$$
$$d\lambda - \lambda\rho dt + [\lambda(t) + d\lambda - \lambda\rho dt]f'(k)dt = 0,$$
$$d\lambda/dt - \lambda\rho + [\lambda(t)]f'(k) = 0,$$

because $[d\lambda - \lambda\rho dt]f'(k)dt$ is of order smaller than dt.

The last equation can be written as

$$f'(k) = \rho - (d\lambda/dt)/\lambda = \rho - (du'(c)/dt)/\lambda = \rho - (dc/dt)[u''(c)/u'(c)],$$

$$or \quad r = \rho + g\eta.$$

The rate of return to capital r equals the discount rate ρ plus the product of the rate of consumption growth $g = (dc/dt)/c$ times the rate of relative risk aversion $\eta = -cu''(c)/u'(c)$. With reasonable estimates of r, ρ and η, the rate of consumption growth, g, is around 1.3% by this equation.

6.4. An Unknown Parameter Leading to Willingness to Sacrifice Much Present Consumption for the Mitigation of Climate Change

When uncertainty is introduced in a parameter of the distribution of the future consumption generated by a stochastic model, Weitzman (2009) shows that the world should be willing to sacrifice much resource for the mitigation of global warming just to raise the utility of one future unit of consumption. I will summarize his argument in an important special case.

Let there be two periods, present and future (about 200 years from now in the discussion of climate change due to the accumulation of CO_2 in the atmosphere) and let the amount of present consumption or output be normalized to equal 1 and the future consumption be C. The stochastic discount factor is defined as

$$M(C) = \beta U'(C)/U'(1). \tag{6.8}$$

It is stochastic because future consumption C is stochastic. Its meaning is clear if we multiply the definition (6.8) by $U'(1)$

$$M(C)U'(1) = \beta U'(C).$$

For any amount of consumption C in the future, the right-hand-side is the discounted utility of one extra unit of future consumption. The left-hand side is the loss of present utility that the utility maximizer is willing to give up to achieve this discounted utility of one future unit of consumption. If the expected value of the stochastic discounted factor is large, the world is willing to give up a lot of present consumption to increase one unit of future consumption.

Assume the utility function

$$U(C) = C^{1-\eta}/(1-\eta); \quad U'(C) = C^{-\eta}. \tag{6.9}$$

To evaluate the expectation of the stochastic factor in the present problem with $U'(C) = C^{-\eta}$ and $C = \exp(Y)$, we write

$$E(M) = \beta E(C^{-\eta}) = \beta E(\exp(-\eta Y)). \tag{6.10}$$

If we know the probability density function of Y, $f(y)$,

$$E(M) = \int \beta e^{-\eta y} f(y) dy. \tag{6.11}$$

Let Y have a normal density function with mean μ and variance s^2, i.e.,

$$f(y) = h(y; s^2) = [1/(2\pi)^{1/2} s] \exp\{-(y-\mu)^2/2s^2\}. \tag{6.12}$$

Substituting this density function in (6.11), we can evaluate $E(M)$ to yield, with $d = -\ln \beta$,

$$E(M) = \exp\{-d - \eta\mu + (1/2)\eta^2 s^2\}. \tag{6.13}$$

If the parameters μ and s^2 of the normal density function are known, we have completed the evaluation of $E(M)$, which is finite.

The problem of uncertainty which Weitzman discusses is the implication for $E(M)$ when μ is known but s^2 is unknown. To evaluate (6.13), we assume a sample of n observations $y_1, \ldots, y_n$ of Y to be given, with its standard deviation denoted by $\nu_n = \Sigma_1^n (y_i - \mu)^2/n$. Let const be a constant number. The likelihood function from the above normal density of y_i is

$$L(s^2; y_1 \ldots y_n) = \text{const}(1/s^n) \exp\{-n\nu_n/2s^2\} = p(\nu_n|s^2), \tag{6.14}$$

which is the conditional density of the data $y_1, \ldots, y_n$ summarized by ν_n given s^2. Let p denote PDF. Equation (6.14) can be written as $p(\nu_n|s^2)$. The joint density of s^2 and ν_n is this conditional density times a prior density $p_0(s^2)$ of s^2. In other words,

$$p(s^2, \nu_n) = p(\nu_n|s^2)\, p_0(s^2).$$

Using a diffuse prior density $p_0(s^2)$ which is proportional to $1/s^2$ and using (6.14) we have

$$p(s^2, \nu_n) = \mathrm{const}(1/s^n) \exp\{-n\nu_n/2s^2\}/s^2.$$

To evaluate the posterior distribution of s^2, change the variable from the variance s^2 to the precision parameter $\theta = 1/s^2$. We can write the joint density of θ and ν_n as, noting the Jacobian to be the absolute value of $ds^2/d\theta = -\theta^{-2}$ or θ^{-2}

$$p(\theta, \nu_n) = \mathrm{const}(\theta^{1+n/2}) \exp\{-n\nu_n\theta/2\}\theta^{-2},$$

which is a gamma density for θ for given ν_n

$$\Gamma(\theta) = \mathrm{const}\,\theta^{\alpha} \exp(-b\theta), \qquad (6.15)$$

where $\alpha = \frac{n}{2} - 1$ and $b = n\nu_n/2$.

To find $f(y)$ in order to evaluate $E(M)$ using (6.11) we use the joint density of y and $\theta = 1/s^2$. This joint density is the product of $h(y; s^2)$ given by (6.12) and the density $\Gamma(\theta)$ given by (6.15), i.e., $[1/(2\pi)^{1/2}s] \exp\{-(y-\mu)^2/2s^2\}\Gamma(\theta)$. We integrate out θ in this joint density to obtain

$$f(y) = \int \mathrm{const}(\theta^{1/2} \exp(-\theta(y-\mu)^2/2))\Gamma(\theta)d\theta, \qquad (6.16)$$

where the integration is from minus infinity to plus infinity. The result of integration gives the Student's t-distribution for y

$$f(y) = \mathrm{const}\left(1 + \frac{(y-\mu)^2}{(n\nu_n)}\right)^{-\frac{(n+2)}{2}}. \qquad (6.17)$$

Using this to evaluate $E(M)$ by (6.11) we find $E(M) = \infty$.

To appreciate Weitzman's derivation, let us review its essential steps

1. The Constant Relative Risk Aversion (CRRA) utility function is used to calculate the stochastic discount factor

$$M = \beta(C^{-\eta}) = \beta\exp(-\eta Y),$$

   making it an exponential function of Y, where Y is $\log(C)$

$$E(M) = \beta E(C^{-\eta}) = \beta E(\exp(-\eta Y)), \qquad (6.10)$$

$$E(M) = \int \beta e^{-\eta y} f(y)\,dy. \qquad (6.11)$$

2. If the density function of Y is normal with variance s^2, $E(M)$ will be an exponential function of s^2

$$E(M) = \exp\{-d - \eta\mu + (1/2)\eta^2 s^2\}. \qquad (6.13)$$

3. If s^2 is unknown and a diffused prior is used, the posterior distribution of $\theta = 1/s^2$ is a gamma distribution

$$\Gamma(\theta) = \text{const}\theta^\alpha \exp(-b\theta), \qquad (6.15)$$

   where $\alpha = \frac{n}{2} - 1$ and $b = n\nu_n/2$.
   The above are three important assumptions used by Weitzman. From these three assumptions, the following two implications follow.

4. The density of Y becomes a t-distribution

$$f(y) = \text{const}\left(1 + \frac{(y - \mu)^2}{(n\nu_n)}\right)^{-\frac{(n+2)}{2}} \qquad (6.17)$$

5. Using the student's t-distribution to evaluate $E(M)$ by Equation (6.11), the result is infinity.

6.5. Why Weitzman's Result is Questionable

Let us first restate the major assumptions in Weitzman's proof. They are

1. Assume the utility function to be $C^{1-\eta}/(1 - \eta)$.
2. Assume normal distribution for $Y = \ln C$.

3. Assume a diffuse prior distribution for the unknown variance s^2 of Y to find a gamma distribution for the posterior distribution of $\theta = 1/s^2$.

Given these three assumptions, two implications follow:

4. Integrate out θ in the joint distribution of y and θ to find $f(y)$ to be a student's t-distribution.
5. Compute the stochastic discount factor using the t-distribution for Y.

The reason why a consumer is willing to sacrifice an unlimited amount of present consumption to avoid the harm of climate change in the future is that the present value of avoiding future climate change is very large, in fact equals infinity. Weitzman has obtained this result by assuming (1) that the distribution of Y, defined by $\log Y$ = consumption C, is normal with a known mean but an unknown variance s^2 and (2) that the prior distribution for the variance s^2 is diffuse. These assumptions lead to a t distribution for the posterior distribution of Y, as given by Equation (6.17). The mean of this t distribution is infinity. Given a utility function which is an increasing function of consumption C and thus of Y, the expected utility of future consumption being sacrificed by global warming is also infinity. Hence the conclusion is reached that the consumer will be willing to sacrifice an infinite amount of present consumption to avoid this infinite amount of future harm. This conclusion is due to the assumption of a diffuse prior for $\theta = 1/s^2$, leading to a posterior t distribution for Y with a mean equal to infinity. This assumption is incorrect because we have prior knowledge today concerning the variance of Y and this variance is finite. Therefore we should reject the unreasonable result that an unlimited amount of resource today should be used to prevent climate change in the future.

On a deeper level one may ask whether statistical inference is applicable to obtain knowledge to decide whether to mitigate the harmful effect of climate change. Statistical analysis requires the quantification of all important information as statistical data. Quantitative measurement is acceptable because we can always pick out something to measure, such as GDP for the economy, log GDP associated with climate change, etc. However, it may not be appropriate to assume a data generating process or assume a probability distribution for the stochastic data representing the above measurements. Furthermore, not all information can be summarized by quantitative measurements.

Bayesian statistics including the use of a diffuse prior is inappropriate because our knowledge about the harmful effect of global warming may not based on statistical data and may not be improved by statistical inference. Tol (2009) points out that the estimates of the harmful effects vary greatly but some are large enough to make us take climate change seriously, thus implying that we should devote resources to mitigate climate change. Unlike Weitzman, Tol does not state that we should devote an infinite amount of resources to mitigate climate change.

In this section I have raised some questions on Weitzman's derivation of the conclusion to mitigate the future harmful effect of climate change at all costs. I do appreciate his ingenuity in demonstrating an interesting proposition by using accepted procedures and assumptions in economic analysis although such procedures may not be appropriate.

References

Chow, G. C. (1997). *Dynamic Economics: Optimization by the Lagrange Method.* Oxford: Oxford University Press.

Sheshinski, Etan (2008). "Comment on the Stern Report," mimeo.

Tol, Richard S. J. (2009). "The Economic Effects of Climate Change," *Journal of Economic Perspectives*, Vol. 23, no. 2 (Spring), pp. 29–51.

Weitzman, Martin L. (2009). "On Modeling and Interpreting the Economics of Catastrophic Climate Change," *Review of Economics and Statistics*, Vol. 91, no. 1, pp. 1–19.

Appendix

Weitzman's Use of his Result to Draw Implications for Climate Change Policy

Can we use a stochastic model for simulation when historical data cannot be assumed to be random drawings from such a model?

It is acceptable to use a mathematical model to summarize our knowledge and deduce implications from it. It is also acceptable to use a stochastic model in which some parameters are uncertain. In this case, we can perform sensitivity analysis of the simulation results for different hypothetical values of the parameters. All this is a thought process without assuming that past data are a random sample from the model. Weitzman's approach requires the scientists who do such stochastic simulations to accept (a) that their knowledge of the parameter values is derived by statistical inference and (b) that they have a flat prior for the unknown parameter(s) to begin with and use Bayesian method to form a posterior of the parameter(s). In other words scientists can use different values of the parameters to do sensitivity analysis of the outcomes from a hypothetical model without accepting a flat tail prior for the parameter(s).

Possible implications for Climate change policy (p. 16 of Weitzman (2009)).
Most existing integrated assessment models (IAMs) for climate change treat forecasts of damages as if they were certain and then do some sensitivity analysis on parameter values. In the rare cases of treating uncertainty, they use thin-tail PDFs, including truncation of PDFs at arbitrary cutoffs. By contrast, this paper has a reduced form with a fat-tailed PDF of $Y = \ln C$.

1. How to map climate change ΔT (low value $2°C-3°C$) to damage in consumption. Economists use $1/[1+\gamma(\Delta T)^2]$. Weitzman uses $\exp(-\gamma(\Delta T)^2)$. Conclusion differs if the latter specification is combined with a fat tailed PDF of ΔT.
2. Simulations with a finite grid may not reveal the true stochastic discounted factor or true discounted expected utility. Weitzman makes two points about the integral

$$E(M) = \beta \int e^{-\eta y} f(y) \, dy. \qquad (6.11)$$

The first is about $f(y)$, which he wants to have a fat tail. The second is the form of the discounted utility $e^{-\eta y}$. Hence "this paper calls for a dramatic oversampling of those stratified climate change scenarios associated with the most adverse imaginable economic impacts in the bad fat tail".

This section of the Weitzman paper is not about implications for climate change policy but about how to perform simulations. I have already pointed out why using Weitzman's fattailed PDF for $Y = \ln C$ for simulation is not a generally accepted methodology used by economists.

Chapter 7
Regional Differences in Environmental Policies

In previous chapters I have confined attention to the analysis of environmental policies for one economy. This chapter deals with environmental policies for two or more economies. Two topics will be discussed. The first is concerned with different policies among nations for CO_2 emission affecting climate change. The second is concerned with differences in amounts of emission of industrial pollutants among different provinces in China. These two problems are conceptually different. In the former, the action of one nation affects the welfare of other nations since the accumulation of CO_2 in the atmosphere affects all nations. In the latter, the action of one province does not affect the welfare of other provinces since effects of industrial pollutants are mainly local. Hence the methods of analysis are different for the two cases. The former requires the use of dynamic game while in the latter the behavior of each province is treated separately. Section 7.1 treats the first problem. The second problem is treated in Sections 7.2 and 7.3.

7.1. Differences in CO_2 Emission Policies Among Nations

Let there be two groups of nations, developing and developed. These nations are concerned with the problem of climate change but have their own perspectives. The developing nations are more concerned with increasing output in the process of economic development while the developed nations are more concerned with a better natural environment since they already have a high level of output for consumption.

It is natural to formulate the model as dynamic game with two players, the first being the developing nations and the second being the developed nations. The dynamic optimization problem for player 1 is expressed by the Lagrangian

$$L_1 = \Sigma\{\beta_1^t[\log(A_1 e_{1t}^{\delta 1}) + \theta_1 \log(M_1 - E_t)]$$
$$- \beta_1^{t+1}\lambda_{t+1}[E_{t+1} - b_1 E_t - b_2 e_{1t} - b_2 e_{2t}]\}. \tag{7.1}$$

This Lagrangian is similar to Equation (3.2) of Chapter 3, except that the control variable is emission e_{1t} of player 1, and the parameters of player 1 are β_1, $\delta 1$, θ_1 and M_1. The emission in year t now consists of e_{1t} and e_{2t}, both appearing in the constraint on the amount E_{t+1} of CO_2 cumulated in the atmosphere at the beginning of year $t+1$ because both contribute to accumulation CO_2 in the atmosphere. Thus the action of player 2 affects the welfare of player 1.

To obtain a Nash equilibrium of this dynamic game, we begin to solve player 1's dynamic optimization problem (7.1) taking the action e_{2t} of player 2 as given. This yields a reaction function for player 1's action e_{1t} as a function of e_{2t}. Similarly we find the reaction function for player 2's action e_{2t} as a function of e_{1t}. In the (e_{1t}, e_{2t}) diagram, an intersection of these two reaction functions is a Nash equilibrium. At a Nash equilibrium when player i chooses his action e_{it} the other player j will choose his action e_{jt} and neither can benefit by deviating from the action specified. The game is dynamic because each player solves a dynamic optimization problem. The solution by the Lagrange method is simple by utilizing the first-order conditions of both players and allowing for their dependence.

For player 1, we maximize β^{-t} times L with respect to the control variable e_{1t} and the state variable E_t, respectively, to yield

$$\delta 1 e_{1t}^{-1} = -b_2 \beta_1 \lambda_{t+1}, \tag{7.2}$$

$$-\theta_1(M_1 - E_t)^{-1} - \lambda_t + b_1 \beta_1 \lambda_{t+1} = 0. \tag{7.3}$$

Using (7.2) to eliminate λ_t and λ_{t+1} in (7.3) we derive player 1's reaction function as

$$-\theta_1(M_1 - E_t)^{-1} + (b_2 \beta_1)^{-1}\delta 1 e_{1,t-1}^{-1} - b_1 b_2^{-1}\delta 1 e_{1t}^{-1} = 0. \tag{7.4}$$

It is interesting to observe that in Equation (7.4) describing the action e_{1t} of player 1, the action e_{2t} of player 2 is absent. The state variable E_t appears in Equation (7.4) for the determination of e_{1t}. Since E_t equals $0.9975\ E_{t-1} + 0.5(e_{1,t-1} + e_{2,t-1})$ the past action $e_{2,t-1}$ of player 2 indirectly affects the current action of player 1 through affecting E_t but even this effect is small because E_t is mainly determined by $0.9975\ E_{t-1}$. The fact that the action of player 2 has almost no effect on the optimal decision of player 1 in the short run also reflects the reality of decision making concerning the regulation of carbon emission among nations. No nation can affect such decision making of other nations on account of its own emission. This point remains valid when we formulate the problem for more than two players using a Lagrangian (1) with e_{3t}, e_{4t}, etc. added to the dynamic constraint for E_{t+1}. Alternatively, one could also consider the decision to regulate carbon emission in a cooperative game.

We solve Equation (7.4) to obtain the action of player 1.

$$-\theta_1 e_{1t} + [(b_2\beta_1)^{-1}\delta 1 e_{1,t-1}^{-1}](M_1 - E_t)e_{1t} - b_1 b_2^{-1}\delta 1(M_1 - E_t) = 0,$$

$$e_{1t} = [(b_2\beta_1)^{-1}\delta 1 e_{1,t-1}^{-1}(M_1 - E_t) - \theta_1]^{-1} b_1 b_2^{-1}\delta 1(M_1 - E_t).$$

$$(7.5)$$

By symmetry, player 2's reaction function is the same except for e_{2t}, β_2, $\delta 2$, θ_2, and M_2 replacing the corresponding variable or parameter for player 1.

To study the differences in emission policies among nations we can consider the actions of the two players at a steady state when $e_{it} = e_i(i = 1, 2)$ remain constant through time. For player 1, Equation (7.5) becomes

$$-\theta_1 e_1 + [(b_2\beta_1)^{-1}\delta 1](M_1 - E_t) - b_1 b_2^{-1}\delta 1(M_1 - E_t) = 0,$$

$$e_1 = \theta_1^{-1} b_2^{-1}\delta 1(\beta_1^{-1} - b_1)(M_1 - E_t).$$

$$(7.6)$$

I use the given parameter values $b_1 = 0.9975$ and $b_2 = 0.5$ for the CO_2 emission case to write (7.6) as

$$e_1 = 2\theta_1^{-1}\delta 1(\beta_1^{-1} - 0.9975)(M_1 - E_t).$$

$$(7.7)$$

Four parameters determine the optimum policy for CO_2 emission for each country. For a poor country represented by player 1, the parameter θ measuring the importance of global warming as represented by the amount of CO_2 in the atmosphere is small. This leads to a larger emission e_1 as given by Equation (7.7). When the future counts less or β_1 is small, the amount of emission e_1 will be large. For these countries, the exponent $\delta 1$ in its Cobb–Douglas production function is larger for the following reason. When only capital and labor are considered as factors of production in a Cobb–Douglas production function, the exponent of capital is large (about 0.6) and the exponent of labor is small (about 0.4) for developing countries as compared with developed economies which have a larger amount of capital relative to labor. (See Mankiw, Romer and Weil 1992; Chow and Lin 2002; and Chow 2015, Chapter 5 for the estimation of the capital exponent in the production function of a developing country.) In the present case, capital is scarce for the developing countries relative to labor. Since carbon emission is associated with the use of capital its exponent is also larger for developing countries. A large $\delta 1$ also leads to a large e_1. Finally, M_1 is also large relative to M_2 because in the utility function of the developing countries, the maximum amount of CO_2 in the atmosphere that can be tolerated is larger.

The above analysis for two players applies to n players since the reaction function of each player is independent of the actions of other players. The reaction function of country i in the steady state is simply Equation (7.7), with subscript i replacing 1. We can therefore apply the theory to explain the policies for CO_2 emission for many countries. If the amounts of CO_2 emission of these n countries represent a Nash equilibrium, no country can deviate from it to make itself better off.

There is another solution concept in game theory known as the dominant-player or the Stackleberg equilibrium. In a Stackleberg equilibrium, player 2, assumed to be the dominant player, will first solve for player 1's action e_1 as a function of his own action e_2. He then takes this function as given and maximizes his utility with respect to e_2. For our problem, the Stackleberg equilibrium turns out to be the same as the Nash equilibrium because the reaction function for player 1 is independent of the action e_2 of player 2. No matter what player 2 does, the action of player 1 remains to be e_1, as given by the Nash equilibrium.

7.2. A Model to Explain Differences in Pollution Among Provinces in China

I will try to apply a similar model to explain differences in air or (in many cases) water pollution among different provinces in China noting that the dynamic equation for the determination of pollution is different. One major change that needs to be made in our model for air pollution in different provinces in China is to assume $b_1 = 0$ and $b_2 = 1$ under the assumption that not much of air pollution in one year remains in the atmosphere in the following year. For water pollution, where pollutants can stay in the water for over one year, we will keep the equation $E_{i,t+1} = b_1 E_{it} + b_2 e_{it}$ for province i.

A second and even more important difference is that air or water pollution mainly stays in the province itself and each province i can be assumed to maximize independently the Lagrangean

$$L_i = \Sigma\{\beta_i^t[\log(A_i e_{it}^{\delta i}) + \theta_i \log(M_i - E_{i,t})]$$
$$-\beta_i^{t+1}\lambda_{t+1}[E_{i,t+1} - b_1 E_{it} - b_2 e_{it}]\}. \tag{7.8}$$

The derivation of the first-order conditions is the same as in Section 7.1, except for the disappearance of the actions of other provinces. Equation (7.6) remains valid for each province. Hence the action of province i is

$$e_{it} = \theta_i^{-1} b_2^{-1} \delta_i (\beta_i^{-1} - b_1)(M_i - E_{it}). \tag{7.9}$$

For the study of air pollution we assume $b_1 = 0$ and $b_2 = 1$. For an approximate solution with $e_{it} = e_{i,i-1} = e_i$ (7.9) becomes

$$e_i = (\beta_i \theta_i + \delta_i)^{-1} \delta_i M_i, \tag{7.10}$$

which is the same equation for the optimum amount of pollution given in Chapter 1 except for the discount factor β_i used to discount the second term $\theta_i \log(M_i - E_{i,t})$ in the utility function, given the fact that the action e_{it} affects the amount of pollution $E_{i,t+1}$ in the future according to the specification of our model.

We take logarithm of (7.10) to obtain

$$\log(e_i) = -log(\beta_i \theta_i + \delta_i) + \log(\delta_i) + \log M_i. \tag{7.11}$$

If Equation (7.11) is to be used to explain the different quantities of air pollutions in China, we must be able to identify provincial characteristics with its parameters $\beta_i, \theta_i, \delta_i$ and M_i. The numerical values of these parameters are unavailable. Hence equation (7.11) cannot be used to explain the quantities of air or water pollution in different provinces in China. Therefore, we need to seek another model.

7.3. A Second Model to Explain Industrial Air Pollution Among Chinese Provinces

I have examined the relation between e (total volume of industrial waste gas emission (100 million cu. m), see *China Environmental Yearbook*) and Y (real GDP) in China for the years 1997–2005 and found the following regression of $\log e$ on $\log Y$:

$$\log(e_t) = -0.4146\,(0.2782) + 1.0664\,(0.0238)\,\log(Y_t); \quad R^2 = 0.9965 \tag{7.12}$$

The theory underlying this regression is the maximization of the utility function

$$\log(Y - \theta e^\gamma) = \log(AK^\alpha L^{1-\alpha}e^\delta - \theta e^\gamma),$$

with respect to e yielding

$$\log(e) = \gamma^{-1}\log(\delta/\theta\gamma) + \gamma^{-1}\log(Y) \tag{7.13}$$

for the relation between $\log e$ and $\log Y$, as also given in equation (4.25). The accompanied scatter diagram is

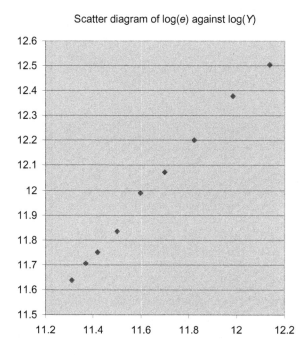

Scatter diagram of log(e) against log(Y)

To understand this relationship in more detail, I decompose e_t in year t into its 31 provincial components $e_{it}(i = 1, 2, \ldots, 31)$. To explain $\log(e_{it}$ per capita) = lec, I use two variables. The first is $\log$(real GDP per capita) = lrgdpc, where real GDP equals provincial nominal GDP divided by provincial CPI. The second is the square of the first variable (lrgdpc)^2 = lrgdpcs. It is introduced to test the environmental Kuznets curve. According to this hypothesis, the effect of the stage of economic development represented by real income per capita on pollution per capita has an inverted U shape. In the course of economic development, the structure of output changes from agriculture to industry and then to services, requiring more and then less use of energy. If the variable (lrgdpc)^2 = lrgdpcs is introduced, its coefficient should be negative.

Before performing the regressions, I first examined the data to find out whether there are outliers and found Tibet's pollution to be especially low. The scatter diagram of log(e) against log(real gdp) is

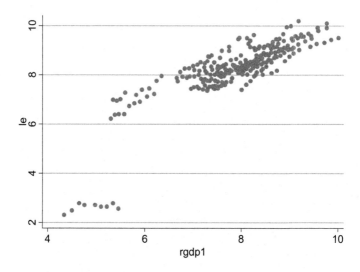

Tibet is shown to be an outlier. Omitting Tibet, the scatter diagram of le against lrgdp becomes

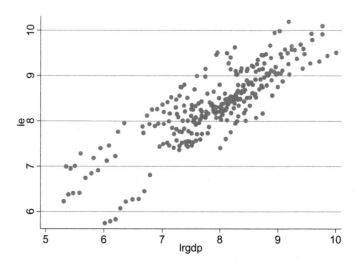

The corresponding scatter diagram of log(e per capita) = lec against log(real GDP per capita) = lrgdpc is

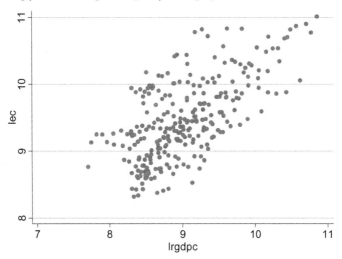

From these two diagrams we can see that the slopes for different provinces appear the same but the intercepts are different. I would like to use these provincial data to find out whether the environmental Kuznets curve EKC has occurred in China.[1] To answer this question I use panel data models that allow for different intercepts for different units (provinces). If we simply estimate a regression using these data without allowing for the different intercepts, the estimated slope will be smaller than if different intercepts are allowed.

An ordinary regression model treats all observations as being generated by

$$Y_{it} = a + b_1 \ x_{1it} + b_2 \ x_{2it} + u_{it}, \tag{7.14}$$

A panel data regression model treats provinces as being different by having their own intercepts

$$Y_{it} = a_i + b_1 \ x_{1it} + b_2 \ x_{2it} + u_{it}. \tag{7.15}$$

The intercepts a_i can be assumed to be random (drawn from a given population) or fixed, resulting in random effect and fixed effect

---

[1]Chapter 10 discusses the EKC in detail.

models respectively. If the intercepts are indeed different, ignoring these differences by using a regression model will lead to specification error and biased estimates of the slopes, as we shall observe below.

An ordinary regression of $\log(e$ per capita$)$ on $\log($real gdp per capita$)$ yields:

$$\log(e/\mathrm{cap}) = 3.6339(0.4146) + 0.6467(0.0458)\log(\mathrm{gdp/cap});$$
$$R^2 = 0.4267; \quad s = 0.4519.$$

The corresponding random effect panel regression of $\log(e$ per capita$)$ on $\log($real gdp per capita$)$ with 270 observations and 30 groups is:

$$\log(e/\mathrm{cap}) = 1.2231(0.3242) + .9135(.0348)\log(\mathrm{gdp/cap});$$
$$R^2: \text{ within} = 0.7430; \text{ between} = 0.3591; \text{ overall} = 0.4267.$$

The panel regression with fixed effect is

$$\log(e/\mathrm{cap}) = 1.0454(0.3208) + 0.9332(0.0355)\log(\mathrm{gdp/cap});$$
$$R^2: \text{ within} = 0.7430; \text{ between} = 0.3591; \text{ overall} = 0.4267.$$

As expected, we observe that the method of ordinary least squares regression underestimates the slope and gives a larger standard error for it as compared with the panel regressions. The results from the two panel regressions with random and fixed effects are very similar.

To test the Kuznets effect using panel regression, I added $[\log(\mathrm{gdp/cap})]^2$ as the second explanatory variable to obtain, for the random effect model, with 270 observations and 30 groups,

$$log(e/\mathrm{cap}) = -3.1420(2.7400) + 1.8747(0.5999)\log(\mathrm{gdp/cap})$$
$$- 0.0527(0.0328)[\log(\mathrm{gdp/cap})]^2; \quad R^2: \text{within} = 0.7462;$$
$$\text{between} = 0.3489; \text{ overall} = 0.4196.$$

The Kuznets effect is partly supported by the negative coefficient of the square variable, which is significant at a 5.4 % level using a one-tail test.

The result from using a fixed effect model is

$$\log(e/\text{cap}) = -3.6168(2.7451) + 1.9603(0.6017)\log(\text{gdp}/\text{cap})$$
$$- 0.0563(0.0329)[\log(\text{gdp}/\text{cap})]^2;$$
$$R^2: \text{within} = 0.7462; \quad \text{between} = 0.3483;$$
$$\text{overall} = 0.419.$$

The result is similar and gives a significant level of 4.45% for the square variable using a one-tail test, confirming the Kuznets effect.

Since income is highly correlated with a time trend t, I also test the significance of time by introducing t as an additional variable and find it to be insignificant. Even when t is included, the square variable remains significant at the 6.65% level.

The conclusion that the coefficient of squared log(real gdp per capita) is negative is subject to question because of the following econometric problems when panel data regressions are applied to estimate and test the parameters of the regressions:

(a) Unit root and spurious correlation. Since the panel data consist of time-series data, econometric problems arising from the study of time series are also problems in dealing with time-series data. The first is the possible existence of unit roots in the process generating the time series Y_{it} and x_{it}. Let these time series be statistically independent but each have a unit root ($Y_{it} = Y_{i,t-1} + u_{it}$; u_{it} serially uncorrelated, and similarly for x_{it}). When we sample these two series and perform a regression of one variable on the other, we are likely to find a coefficient that is statistically different from zero by an ordinary t-test. Each of the two variables is said to have a stochastic trend, and the observed correlation between them is said to be spurious. Standard regression analysis cannot be applied to such time series.

(b) Testing for unit roots and for the order of integration and the use of regression analysis for variables of the same order of integration. If the existence of unit roots creates a serious problem, a researcher should test whether unit roots exist in the data. If no unit root exists, the objection given by (a) will not create a problem. Testing for unit roots is often inconclusive partly because the result depends on the null hypothesis chosen for the regression coefficient β in the model $Y_{it} = \beta Y_{i,t-1} + u_{it}$. If the null hypothesis is the existence of a unit root, namely $\beta = 1$, a test may not reject it. If the null hypothesis is $\beta = 0.98$, it will not be rejected either. If we conclude that unit roots exist in the data, we next find the order of integration of each time series. The order of integration is zero, if it is stationary. The order is one if it becomes a stationary series after taking first difference and is two if it becomes stationary after taking second difference, etc. If a linear relation of two time series each having order of integration of one is itself stationary, the two time series are said to be cointegrated. In this case, a least-squares regression of one series on the other will give a consistent estimate of the true slope of the underlying linear function (see Engle and Granger (1987)). A main objection of Romero–Avila (2008) to many studies of the EKC is that Y and x have different orders of cointegration and hence regression analysis will not yield consistent estimate of the slope of the linear relation.

(c) Heteroskedicity (or unequal variances of u_{it}), serial dependence and correlation across countries in the residuals u_{it} in Equation (7.15). All these problems affect the validity of the t-test for the regression coefficients.

(d) There may be breaking points in the model, especially in the coefficient γ, which need to be tested as suggested by Romero–Avila (2008). When there are breaking points, the treatment of panel data models with data of different order of integration becomes complicated as pointed out by Perron (1989).

(e) Simultaneous-equations bias or possible correlation between u_{it} and the included explanatory variables in (7.15). This can happen if there are explanatory variables for Y_{it} which we have omitted in (7.15). Unlike the econometric problems raised in (a) to (d), we consider this problem irrelevant for our definition of the EKC as specified by Equation (7.15). Our specification of the EKC requires us to estimate relationship (7.15) without including other explanatory variables, although including them would change the coefficients in (7.15). If there were other important variables correlated with the included explanatory variables in (7.15) they are irrelevant because the hypothesis is about the relation (7.15). To put this in another way, let there be a trivariate normal distribution for x, y and z and we are interested in a simple regression of y on x. We should go ahead to estimate this simple regression by the method of least squares without including z. Of course including z would change the coefficient of x but that is not the coefficient of interest to us and the regression including z is not what we want.

Given these econometric problems, I propose to use a statistical test of the null hypothesis that a coefficient in a panel data regression is zero against the alternative hypothesis that it is negative by using a simple t-test. This t-test is performed as follows. Assume that we have data for all variables for $i = 1, 2, \ldots, n$ and $t = 1, 2, \ldots, T$. For each year t, we perform a regression to estimate the Kuznets equation using data for the n countries and obtain an estimate c_t of the coefficient of the squared term for $t = 1, \ldots, T$. We then use a t statistic to test the null hypothesis that $c_t (t = 1, 2, \ldots, T)$ come from a population with mean 0 against the alternative hypothesis that the mean is negative. This test is valid provided that the c_t for different t are statistically independent or nearly so.

Note that this test avoids all the time-series problems possibly occurring when we treat (7.15) as a panel data model by combining all observations for n countries in T periods. By using a panel data regression for all available data one would encounter all the time series problems (a), (b) and (c) stated earlier. The t-test employed is not based on any regression using time-series data. Each regression is a cross-section regression. The only problem is that in the regression for each period t using data for different provinces the residuals are correlated, but in this case an ordinary least squares estimate is still unbiased, although an estimate by the method of generalized least squares would be more efficient. For our t-test we need only to have each estimate c_t of the coefficient of the squared term to be unbiased for all t. The same comment applies to possibly heterogeneous u_{it}.

Concerning possible problem (d), our null hypothesis is to test the mean of c_t being zero. There may be gradual shift or structural breaks in the other coefficients in (7.15), which do not concern us. If there were shifts in the coefficient of the squared term of the Kuznets equation itself, our null hypothesis is that $c_t (t = 1, 2, \ldots, T)$ have the same population mean and shifts in the population mean will be detected by the t-test that all means are zero.

This t-test was used by Fama and MacBeth (1973) for testing the CAPM model in finance using data of different firms or stocks as individual units. Cross-section regressions for different years were estimated separately, and a t-test was applied to the resulting yearly coefficients. Ibragimov and Müller (2010) provide a theoretical justification of this test.

To apply the above t-test, I have performed nine cross-section regressions using provincial data for the nine years from 1997 to 2005. The nine coefficients of log(gdp per capita) squared and their t statististics in parentheses are 0.3912967 (1.65), 0.4131993 (1.83), 0.4199115 (1.97), 0.4044062 (2.00), 0.2805594 (1.51), 0.2518759 (1.29), 0.1703233 (0.81), 0.0724902 (0.34), and -0.2055744 (-0.84). Note that most of these coefficients are positive and their mean is 0.2442765. To test the null hypothesis that their population mean is zero, we compute the t-statistic to be 3.5271, with eight degrees of freedom, leading to rejecting null hypothesis and accepting the alternative hypothesis that it is positive at the 0.0039 level of significance. Thus in the years 1997 to 2005 used for the t test, China definitely did not reach the downward sloping part of the environmental Kuznets curve. Nevertheless, this result does not contradict the Environmental Kuznets curve for China because, in the future, after China shall have become a developed economy, the data may show a coefficient of log(real gdp) squared being negative. The evidence only shows that the declining part of the EKC has not yet arrived in China.

References

Chow, Gregory C. (2015). *China's Economic Transformation.* 3rd edn., UK: Wiley. Forthcoming.

Chow, Gregory and Anloh Lin (2002). "Accounting for Economic Growth for Taiwan and Mainland China: A Comparative Analysis," *Journal of Comparative Economics*, Vol. 30, pp. 507–530.

Engle, R. F. and Granger, C. W. J. (1987). "Cointegration and Error Correction: Representation, Estimation, and Testing," *Econometrica*, 55, 251–276.

Fama, E. and J. MacBeth (1973). "Risk, Return and Equilibrium: Empirical Tests," *Journal of Political Economy*, 81(3), 607–636

Ibragimov, Rustam and Ulrich K. Müller (2010). "t-Statistic Based Correlation and Heterogeneity Robust t Inference," *Journal of Business & Economic Statistics*.

Mankiw, N. Gregory, David Romer and David N. Weil (1992). "The Empirics of Economic Growth," *Quarterly Journal of Economics*, Vol. 108, pp. 407–438.

Perron, P. (1989). "The Calculation of the Limiting Distribution of the Least-squares Estimator in a Near-Integrated Model," *Econometric Theory*, 5, 1361–401.

Romero-Avila, D. (2008) "Questioning the Empirical Basis of the Environmental Kuznets Curve for CO_2: New Evidence from a Panel Stationarity Test Robust to Multiple Breaks and Cross-dependence," *Ecological Economics*, 64(3), 559–574.

Chapter 8

Macroeconomic Models to Explain Pollution and Environmental Protection

In this chapter, I first present a macroeconomic model incorporating the use of energy in production and capital accumulation in Section 8.1. This model differs from the model of Section 4.5 in having a maximum tolerable level M for emission in the utility function. It is used to explain the reduction of the consumption/output ratio observed from Chinese data. In Section 8.2, a production function with energy as input is estimated using panel data for developing countries in Asia. Section 8.3 presents a model to explain the protection of environment by introducing a variable s for scrubbing. Section 8.4 presents a market solution of the model of Section 8.3, which solves the model as a problem of dynamic optimization on the part of a hypothetical central planner.

8.1. A Dynamic Model to Explain Pollution and Rate of Consumption Growth

In this section, I discuss a macroeconomic model incorporating the choice of output and clean environment as another generalization of the basic model of Chapter 1. It differs from the model of Section 4.2 by treating the use of energy as an input in the aggregate production function, under the simplifying assumption that e represents both energy use and emission. This introduces e as an additional control variable.

Let the central planner maximize the following Lagrangean

$$L = \sum_t \{\beta^t [\log C_t + \theta \log(M - e_t)$$
$$- \beta \lambda_{t+1}[K_{t+1} - (1 - d)K_t - Y_t + C_t]\}. \tag{8.1}$$

Here aggregate output Y is assumed to be produced by the production function $Y_t = a_t K_t^\gamma L_t^{1-\gamma} e_t^\delta$. I treat e_t as the amount of energy required in the production of Y and define energy in the same unit as emission or pollution. The dynamic constraint in (8.1) states that output Y equals consumption C plus the accumulation of capital $K_{t+1} - (1 - d)K_t$. The control variables are C_t and e_t and the state variable is K_t. Differentiating (8.1) with respect to C_t, e_t and K_t, respectively, for each period t yields

$$C_t^{-1} = \beta\lambda_{t+1}, \tag{8.2}$$

$$-\theta/(M - e_t) + \beta\delta Y_t e_t^{-1}\lambda_{t+1} = 0 \tag{8.3}$$

$$-\lambda_t + (1 - d)\beta\lambda_{t+1} + \gamma Y_t K_t^{-1}\beta\lambda_{t+1} = 0. \tag{8.4}$$

Using (8.2) to substitute C for λ in (8.3) and (8.4) gives

$$-\theta/(M - e_t) + \delta Y_t e_t^{-1} C_t^{-1} = 0, \tag{8.3a}$$

$$-\beta^{-1}C_{t-1}^{-1} + C_t^{-1}[(1 - d) + \gamma Y_t K_t^{-1}] = 0, \tag{8.4a}$$

which imply, respectively,

$$-\theta e_t + \delta Y_t C_t^{-1}(M - e_t) = 0; \quad e_t = \delta M/(\theta C_t/Y_t + \delta), \tag{8.5}$$

$$C_t = \beta[1 - d + \gamma Y_t K_t^{-1}]C_{t-1}. \tag{8.6}$$

Equation (8.5) is an equation explaining the demand for energy or emission e_t. If in the Lagrangean (8.1) the term e^δ in the production function for Y disappears and $K_{t+1} = K_t$ this model is reduced to the static model with $C_t = Y_t$, and the optimum e_t given by Equation (8.5) becomes $e_t = \delta M/(\theta + \delta)$, which is identical to the result of Equation (1.2) for the static model of Chapter 1. In the present dynamic model since $Y_t^{-1}C_t$ is smaller than 1, the solution for e_t given by Equation (8.5) becomes larger than the static case. The reason is that when a part of output is devoted to capital accumulation, less is available for current consumption. When consumption of physical good is reduced consumption of clean environment $(M - e)$ will also be reduced to balance the two marginal utilities. In other words, pollution will increase.

In the course of economic development, when pollution e_t increases before reaching the limit M, by Equation (8.5) C_t/Y_t has to decrease.

This implication agrees with the Chinese data on the reduction of the consumption/GDP ratio as presented in Table 4.2. Thus our model can explain the increase in pollution and the reduction in the ratio C/Y in China during the period 1997 to 2005. However, the increasing trend for e and the decreasing trend in the ratio C_t/Y_t cannot continue indefinitely because of the upper limit M for e. When e stays constant before reaching the upper limit M, the ratio C/Y will also stay constant at the later stage of economic development.

Equation (8.6) is the same as Equation (4.6) of Chapter 4, which explains the evolution of consumption over time. In Section 4.2, we assumed $e_t = cY_t$, and $Y_t = a_t K_t^\gamma L_t^{1-\gamma}$, i.e., energy is not a factor of production but output Y generates e = emission = pollution. Now we assume e_t = energy to be a factor of production in $Y_t = a_t K_t^\gamma L_t^{1-\gamma} e_t^\delta$ but no equation explaining the production of energy itself. However, the consumption Equation (8.6) remains the same but we now have Equation (8.5) to explain the evolution of emission or the use of energy e_t. I now turn to the estimation of the production function.

8.2. Estimation of a Production Function with Energy as Input Using Data for Asian Economies

Let Y_{it} be real GDP of country i in period t, K_{it} be capital stock, L_{it} be labor and e_{it} be the amount of energy used in production. Given data on these variables estimate the regression

$$\log Y_{it} = a_i + b \log K_{it} + c \log L_{it} + d \log e_{it} + g_i t + u_{it},$$

where a_i (or $\exp(a_i)$) measures the level of technology of country i, u_{it} measures the efficiency of country i in period t and g_i is the percentage rate of technological change for country i.

Given a_i, K_{it}, L_{it}, t and u_{it} we have a relationship $\log Y_{it} = d \log e_{it} + k_{it}$. For simplicity, the amount of pollutants emitted is also denoted by e_{it}. If we measure $\log Y_{it}$ along the y-axis and $\log e_{it}$ along the x-axis, we have a straight line with intercept k_{it} (a linear function of all other variables in the above regression) and slope d. This means that the use of energy is required to produce output Y_{it}.

We can estimate the above equation or variants of it (such as allowing d to depend on i; b and c will also depend on i if the sample includes developed and developing countries but not when all countries are developing countries). In the paper *"On the Empirics Of Economic Growth,"* Mankiw *et al.* (1992) find the same capital exponent b to be about 0.6 for all developing countries in their sample. If we have both developing and developed countries, we may have to assume b and c to be the same only for one group of countries.

The following results are obtained using the data from 1980 to 1995 for 11 Asian economies, including China, Hong Kong, India, Indonesia, Japan, Korea, Malaysia, Philippines, Singapore, Taiwan and Thailand, used by the Jeon and Sickles (2004).

To examine the nature of the data, I first regress $\log(y) = \log(\text{gdp})$ on $\log K$, $\log L$ and time t. The following result is reasonable. The coefficient of $\log K$ is not very far from 0.6. This result is in agreement with the 0.6 estimates reported in Chapter 4 of *China's Economic Transformation* (Chow, 2015).

$$\log y = \text{con} + 0.684(0.017)\log K + 0.227(0.012)\log L$$
$$+ 0.0044(0.0027)t; \quad R^2/s = 0.9859/0.1538.$$

The two panel regressions below, the first assuming random effect and the second assuming fixed effect, also support the capital exponent being approximately equal to 0.6.

$$\log y = \text{con} + 0.658(0.042)\log K + 0.231(0.037)\log L$$
$$+0.0063(0.0029)t; \quad \text{R-sq : within} = 0.9428;$$
$$\text{between} = 0.9883; \quad \text{overall} = 0.9859.$$

$$\log y = \text{con} + 0.452(0.061)\log K + 0.185(0.041)\log L$$
$$+0.266(0.059)\log e + 0.0054(0.0029)t;$$
$$\text{R-sq : within} = 0.9510; \quad \text{between} = 0.9764;$$
$$\text{overall} = 0.9750.$$

The assumption that $\log(CO_2)$ and $\log(\text{energy})$ are identical made in this chapter is supported by the following scatter diagram.

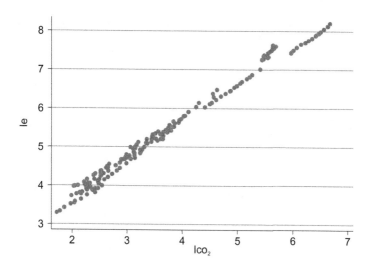

Hence, we can replace log (energy) by log (CO_2) to re-estimate the regression explaining log (GDP). The result below is excellent. The estimate of the coefficient of $\log(CO_2)$ 0.2539 (0.0449) is similar to the coefficient of log(energy) 0.2660 (0.0590) but with an even larger t ratio of 5.655 as compared with 4.508.

$$\log y = \text{con} + 0.483(0.051)\log K + 0.168(0.041)\log L$$
$$+0.254(0.045)\log(CO_2) + 0.0052(0.0028)t;$$
$$\text{R-sq} : \text{within} = 0.9540; \quad \text{between} = 0.09754;$$
$$\text{overall} = 0.9743.$$

This regression shows that, given e, output y can be increased by increasing the other factors of production. Hence by increasing the other factors of production energy intensity (the energy to output ratio) can be reduced (see Jean and Sickles, 2001). We will not use nonlinear regression to estimate the parameters M and θ in equation (8.5) to explain emission e as a similar exercise was performed in Section 4.3. Instead we turn our attention to explain scrubbing as a means to reduce emission or pollution in the next section.''

8.3.   A Model to Explain the Protection of Environment by Srubbing

In this model we introduce the control variable s_t (for scrubbing) in order to explain the amount spent on protection of the environment. By allowing for the possibility to protect the environment economic growth can be sustained. Let g denote the cost per unit of scrubbing s. The Lagrangean for the central planner is

$$L = \sum_t \{\beta^t [\log C_t + \theta \log(M - e_t + s_t)$$
$$- \beta\lambda_{t+1}[K_{t+1} - (1-d)K_t - Y_t + C_t + gs_t]\}. \tag{8.7}$$

Note the tradeoff in using output Y to increase utility by scrubbing to have a cleaner environment or for consumption C in the dynamic constraint. Differentiating (8.7) with respect to C_t, e_t, s_t and K_t, respectively, for each period t yields

$$C_t^{-1} = \beta\lambda_{t+1}, \tag{8.8}$$

$$-\theta/(M - e_t + s_t) + \beta\delta Y_t e_t^{-1}\lambda_{t+1} = 0, \tag{8.9}$$

$$\theta/(M - e_t + s_t) - \beta g\lambda_{t+1} = 0, \tag{8.9a}$$

$$-\lambda_t + (1-d)\beta\lambda_{t+1} + \gamma Y_t K_t^{-1}\beta\lambda_{t+1} = 0. \tag{8.10}$$

Using (8.8) to substitute C for λ in (8.9), (8.9a) and (8.10) gives

$$-\theta/(M - e_t + s_t) + \delta Y_t e_t^{-1}C_t^{-1} = 0, \tag{8.9'}$$

$$\theta/(M - e_t + s_t) - gC_t^{-1} = 0, \tag{8.9a'}$$

$$-\beta^{-1}C_{t-1}^{-1} + C_t^{-1}[(1-d) + \gamma Y_t K_t^{-1}] = 0. \tag{8.10'}$$

Equations (8.9') and (8.9a') imply $g = \delta Y_t e_t^{-1}$ or

$$e_t = (\delta/g)Y_t. \tag{8.11}$$

Equations (8.9a') and (8.11) imply

$$s_t = g^{-1}(\theta + \delta)(C_t + Y_t) - M \tag{8.11a}$$

Equation (8.10′) implies

$$C_t = \beta[1 - d + \gamma Y_t K_t^{-1}]C_{t-1}. \tag{8.12}$$

Equation (8.11a) expresses s_t as a linear function of $(C_t + Y_t)$. Consumption can keep on increasing as long as s_t increases to protect the environment. Equations (8.11), (8.11a) and (8.12) can all be estimated.

8.4. Market Solution of the Model of Section 8.3

In this section I will show that the solution derived in Section 8.3 by the central planner maximizing utility subject to a dynamic constraint can be derived in a market economy with consumers maximizing utility subject to a budget constraint and produces maximizing profits. If this is the case, the market economy is efficient, working as efficiently as a central planner who is all-knowing (knowing the representative consumer's utility function and the representative firm's production function).

The representative consumer owns capital stock equal to K, labor equal to L and the natural environment, which enables him to sell emission permits e to producers who use natural resource e to produce using a production function $Y = Y(K, L, e)$. The return to capital is r; the wage rate is w and the price of emission permits is q. Thus his income is $Y = rK + wL + qe$. The consumer desires clean air and is willing to pay a price g per unit of scrubbing by a producer. There is a constant-cost technology to clean the air at g per unit. Hence g is given in the model. The consumer's income Y is spent for consumption C, buying clean air gs and saving $K_{t+1} - K_t$ as specified in the dynamic constraint in the Lagrangean expression below. His control variables are C, e and s, and his state variable is K.

The representative consumer maximizes the Lagrangean expression

$$L = \sum_t \{\beta^t [\log C_t + \theta \log(M - e_t + s_t) - \beta^{t+1}\lambda_{t+1}[K_{t+1} \\ - (1 - d)K_t + C_t + g_t s_t - r_t K_t - w_t L_t - q_t e_t]]\},$$

with respect to C, e, s and K, yielding, respectively,

$$C_t^{-1} = \beta \lambda_{t+1}, \tag{8.13}$$

$$\theta/(M - e_t + s_t) = q_t \beta \lambda_{t+1}, \tag{8.14}$$

$$\theta/(M - e_t + s_t) = g_t \beta \lambda_{t+1}, \tag{8.15}$$

$$\lambda_t = (1 - d + r_t)\beta \lambda_{t+1} \quad \beta^{-1} C_{t-1}^{-1} = (1 - d + r_t)C_t^{-1}$$

$$C_t = (1 - d + r_t)\beta C_{t-1}. \tag{8.16}$$

Equation (8.13) is used to replace $\beta \lambda_{t+1}$ by C_t^{-1}. Equations (8.14) and (8.15) imply $q_t = g_t$. Also, only one equation remains for the determination of the variable $(e - s)$. Given C_{t-1}, we have Equation (8.16) to determine C_t and Equation (8.14) or (8.15) to determine the net supply $(e - s)$ for a given price $q = g$. Solving this equation, we have the following equation to determine the net emission $(e - s)$:

$$C_t \theta = q_t (M - e_t + s_t). \tag{8.17}$$

This equation shows that the net supply of emission $(e - s)$ increases with price q.

The representative producer is assumed to maximize profit, which equals

$$aK^\gamma L^{1-\gamma} e^\delta - rK - wL - qe$$

Differentiating with respect to K, L and e yields, respectively

$$r = \gamma Y/K, \tag{8.18}$$

$$w = (1 - \gamma)Y/L, \tag{8.19}$$

$$q = \delta Y/e. \tag{8.20}$$

Since K and L are known, the production function $Y = Y(K, L, e)$, the national income identity $Y = rK + wL + qe$, and Equations (8.18), (8.19) and (8.20) provide five equations to determine the five unknowns r, w, q, Y and e. Equation (8.20) agrees with Equation (8.11) of Section 8.3 and states that emission is proportional to output, $e = (\delta/q)Y$. Equation (8.16) is the same as

Equation (8.12) of Section 8.3 once the right-hand side of (8.18) is used to replace r.

In the last two sections, we have provided a theory to explain scrubbing. Econometric analysis remains a topic of future research. *China Statistical Yearbook* has a chapter on energy and data are available to estimate an equation for total expenditure to clean up the environment in China.

References

Chow, Gregory C. (2015). *China's Economic Transformation*, 3rd edn., UK: Wiley. Forthcoming.

Jeon, Byung M. and Robin C. Sickles (2004). "The Role of Environmental Factors in Growth Accounting." *Journal of Applied Econometrics*, 19, 567–591.

Mankiw, N., Romen, D., and Weih, D. (1992). "On the Empirics of Economic Growth," *Quarterly Journal of Economics*, 107, 407–38.

Questions

1. Generalize the model of Section 8.1 to allow for the accumulation of pollution satisfying the dynamic equation $E_{t+1} - b_1 E_t - b_2 e_t = 0$. Solve for and interpret the first-order conditions of dynamic optimization.

2. Provide a market solution to the model of question 1.

3. Based on the model of Section 8.1, is it possible to reduce the energy output ratio (energy intensity) by increasing the other factors of production? See Jeon--Sickles paper in *Journal of Applied Econometrics*.

4. What is missing in the model of Section 8.1 as compared with the Jeon--Sickles paper in the *Journal of Applied Econometrics*?

Chapter 9
Use of Emission Permits

9.1. Introduction

To control the amount of pollution or emission of pollutants, two types of methods have been used. One is command and control, which prohibits or limits the amount of pollution by each potential polluter. The second method relies on economic incentives. It makes a polluter pay according to the amount of pollutants emitted. This may take the form of taxing the polluter according to the amount of emission. It may take the form of requiring the polluters to pay for emission permits per unit of emission. The price of permits may be fixed by the regulator. It may also be determined by the market forces of demand and supply when the permits can be traded. This chapter deals with the use of emission permits to regulate emission.

A main idea of this book is to treat the problem of pollution and carbon emission as the use of underpriced natural resource that leads to wastes and inefficiency. A solution proposed is to price the natural sources correctly. The use of emission permits can lead to the correct pricing of the otherwise underpriced natural resource. If the resources are owned by private owners, the owners would have the incentive to charge the correct price provided a set of market institutions exists. In Chapter 2, we have presented a proposal for the regulation of industrial air or water pollution in China, which utilizes emission permits as a means to control the amount of emission. In the case of pollution in China, the representatives of Chinese citizens act on behalf of the owner-citizens to decide on the total number of permits to issue. In the case of the control of carbon emission through the UN, I will propose in Section 9.5 that the General Assembly takes a median vote to decide on the total amount of emission allowed. In both cases, emission permits are used. These emission permits can be traded to achieve a Pareto optimum, as trade can improve the welfare of the parties concerned.

This chapter provides an economic analysis of emission permits by considering the demand for and supply of the use of an underpriced natural resource that generates emission e. Section 9.2 is a static analysis. Section 9.3 is a dynamic analysis of the demand and supply of the underpriced natural resource. Section 9.4 introduces to the reader a general equilibrium analysis of the production and consumption of a product in which carbon emission occurs and the producers are required to obtain emission permits that can be traded. Section 9.5 discusses the regulation of carbon emission in the world by the use of emission permits and associated problems.

9.2. Static Analysis of the Demand for and Supply of an Underpriced Input

Imagine electricity being produced by one company in a city or town by a monopoly, and assume that there are a number of towns in an economy. In the production process, there is externality because carbon is emitted. The city government wants the electricity producer to obtain a permit for the carbon emitted. Consider first the market equilibrium under monopolistic competition, with each producer or firm facing a negatively sloping demand curve for its product. Profit maximization by the firm yields a demand for input equation. Imposing a charge to this input will reduce its use. If the same charge is imposed for all producers for the use of this input, they all pay the same marginal cost for this input. Equalization of the marginal costs among the users will lead to a Pareto optimum in the allocation of the scarce natural resource. These ideas will be developed in this section using a specific production function and a specific demand function for the output of the producer or firm.

Let the firm have a production function as specified in previous chapters, namely,

$$y = AK^\gamma L^\beta e^\delta,$$

with y, K, L and e denoting output, capital, labor and a natural input that is measured by the amount e emitted. When capital and labor are treated as fixed in the short run, the production is simply written as

$$y = Ae^{\delta}.$$

In order to use the natural input e the firm is required to pay a price q per unit. In Section 1.3 of Chapter 1, we studied the demand for e by a firm that can sell the output at a constant price of unity and the supply of e by consumers who maximize utility. The firm is now assumed to face a negatively sloping linear demand equation with the price of its output denoted by p

$$p = a - by,$$

and to maximize profit when the cost of the natural input e is q per unit. Given

$$\text{profit} = pAe^{\delta} - eq = (a - by)y - eq = ay - by^2 - eq,$$

the firm will maximize $ay - by^2 - qe$ with respect to e by setting to zero its derivative with respect to e to obtain the first-order condition for maximum, with y' denoting the derivative of $y = Ae^{\delta}$ with respect to e, $\delta Ae^{\delta-1}$,

$$(a - 2by)y' = q.$$

The demand equation for e is negatively sloping if the left-hand-side of the above equation has a negative derivative with respect to y since y' is positive. Given a positive y', the derivative of the left-hand side with respect to y is $-2b$, which is certainly negative. If the supply of e owned by the consumers is as given in Section 1.3, the amount of e is determined by equating supply and demand as in Section 1.3.

Since demand for input is set to a point where the marginal revenue product equals the price, when this condition is satisfied for every firm that produce electricity for the economy, the marginal revenue product of the natural resource will be equalized. Any reallocation among producers will lead to a deviation from Pareto optimum. It is in this sense that the use of emission permits will lead to a Pareto optimum allocation of the scarce natural input provided all producers pay the same price for the permits. Whatever the initial amounts are allocated to different firms, if the firms are permitted to trade the permits, the prices of all permits will be equal and the Pareto optimum allocation of this input will be achieved.

If the natural input is not owned by the consumers, the government wishing to regulate emission has to determine the total quantity of permits to be issued, or the total carbon allowed to be emitted in the atmosphere in the case of the control of carbon emission. In the proposal that I made for the regulation of air or water pollution as discussed in Chapter 2, I suggested that the representives of the Chinese people living in the community affected by the polluted air or water decide the total amount. The decision presumably balances the advantage of having cleaner air or water and the disadvantage of having less output produced in the community. In the proposal that I will make for the regulation of carbon emission through the United Nations, member nations take a median vote on the total amount to be emitted. The votes will depend on a nation's wish to trade off less output for less carbon in the atmosphere.

9.3. Dynamic Analysis of Emission Permits

This book has provided a number of dynamic models in which the control of pollution or the limitation of the use of a natural resource plays an important role. In the present context, we need to model the dynamic optimization for the firms producing an output like electricity while using as an input a natural resource that needs to be priced.

We can set up the firm's problem as maximizing a discounted sum of profits over time given its production function that requires an input e given a price q per unit of this input. In the special case, the price q can be zero if the natural resource is free. One simple case is to assume that q is constant over time. In that case the profit function of each firm is

$$\sum_t \beta^t [p_t y_t - q_t e_t] = \sum_t \beta^t [(a - b y_t) y_t - q_t e_t] = \sum_t \beta^t [a y_t - b y_t^2 - q_t e_t],$$

where $y_t = A e_t^\delta$ if we assume the production function to be constant over time. The solution to the demand equation for the natural input will be the same as given in Section 9.2. Pareto optimum will be achieved in every period.

This treatment of a dynamic model that yields solutions identical with the solution of a simple static model has other examples in this book. For example in Section 7.2, the dynamic model to explain differences in pollution among provinces in China implies a one-period solution identical with the equilibrium condition for the optimum level of pollution or emission of the simple model in Section 1.2, except for the discount factor used to discount future utility.

Although the first-order conditions derived from a dynamic model may be identical with those derived from a static model, dynamic models are needed when there are important tradeoff in the use of economic resources overtime. For example, in the treatment of investment and capital formation, there is a trade-off between more consumption today and capital formation to increase consumption in the future. In the discussion of environmental problems, the discount rate is important in deciding whether resources should be used to increase consumption today or for prevention of environmental degradation, which affects output and consumption in the future.

9.4. A General Equilibrium Analysis of Trading of Emission Permits

The purpose of this section is to introduce a paper Carmona *et al.* (2010), which provides a general equilibrium dynamic analysis of emission permits using the allocation to producers of electricity in the European countries as a motivating example. The authors state in the abstract:

> We propose a model for an economy where risk neutral firms produce goods to satisfy an inelastic demand and are endowed with permits in order to offset their pollution at compliance time and avoid having to pay a penalty. Firms that can easily reduce emissions do so, while those for which it is harder buy permits from firms which anticipate they will not need all their permits, creating a financial market for pollution credits. Our equilibrium model elucidates the joint price formation for goods and pollution allowances, capturing most of the features of the first

phase of the European Union Emissions Trading Scheme. We show existence of an equilibrium and uniqueness of emissions credit prices. We also characterize the equilibrium prices of goods and the optimal production and trading strategies of the firms.

The mathematical tools used are much more sophisticated insofar as stochastic process in discrete time is employed. Some assumptions are introduced that are questionable. First, demand for electricity is assumed to be inelastic, whereas the treatments in Sections 9.2 and 9.3 allow the demand for electricity to depend on the price of electricity. Second, all firms are assumed to make their decisions with a finite time horizon of a specific number of time periods. Our analyses cover the case of one period, or the static case, and the dynamic case of an infinite time horizon. This somewhat arbitrary assumption is introduced perhaps to enable the authors to arrive at a general equilibrium for the stochastic processes introduced. The analysis is broader than the analyses given in Sections 9.2 and 9.3 in treating a financial market for pollution credits. The multiperiod setup of this paper allows the trading of emission permits in the future as the firms consider the need for future permits up to the end of the finite time horizon.

As a motivation of their paper, the authors write

> At the time of the writing of the first version of the paper, the two most prominent examples of existing cap-and-trade systems are the EU-ETS (European Union Emission Trading Scheme) and the US Sulfur Dioxide Trading System. In such systems, a central authority sets a limit (cap) on the total amount of pollutant that can be emitted within a pre-determined period. To ensure that this target is complied with, a certain number of credits are allocated to appropriate installations and a penalty is applied as a charge per unit of pollutant emitted outside the limits. Firms may either reduce their own pollution or purchase emission credits in anticipation of potentially significant penalties. This transfer of allowances by trading is considered to be the core principle leading to the minimization of the costs caused by regulation; companies that can easily reduce emissions will do so, while those for which it is harder buy credits.

The discussions of Sections 9.2 and 9.3 apply to the institutional setting of the EU-ETS (European Union Emission Trading Scheme) and the US Sulfur Dioxide Trading System as well. While the authors mention the "minimization of cost caused by the regulation," we note the principle of achieving a Pareto optimum because each firm pays the same marginal cost of using the scarce natural capital. This statement can be made without requiring a proof of the existence of equilibrium in each specific economic application.

To illustrate the kind of modeling presented in the paper by Carmona *et al.*, consider the very simple introductory example used to illustrate their model at the beginning of their discussion before their elaborate model is introduced.

Let us consider a set of firms that must satisfy a demand of $D = 1\,\mathrm{MWh}$ of electricity at each time $t = 0, 1, \ldots, T - 1$ and let us assume that there are only two possible technologies to produce electricity: gas technology which has unit cost 2 \$ and emits 1 ton of CO_2 per MWh produced, and coal technology which has unit cost 1 \$ and emits 2 tons of CO_2 per MWh. In this simple model, the total capacity of gas is 1 MWh and the total capacity of coal is also 1 MWh. We also suppose that producers face a penalty of \$ π per ton of CO_2 not offset by credits, and that a total of $T - 1$ credits are distributed to the firms, allowing them to offset altogether $T - 1$ tons of CO_2. Here π is a number strictly greater than 1. In this situation, we arrive at two conclusions. First, as demand needs to be met, total emissions will be greater than or equal to T tons, even if all firms use the clean technology (gas). Second, firms are always better off reducing emissions than paying the penalty. As a consequence, the optimal generation strategy is to only use gas technology and emit T tons of CO_2. At least one firm has to pay the penalty and the price of emission credits is necessarily equal to π at each time. The missing credit has a value π for both the buyer and the seller, so the price of electricity is $2 + \pi$ because a marginal decrease in demand will induce a marginal gain in generation cost and a marginal decrease in penalty paid. The total profit for the producers is $\pi(T - 1)$, the penalty paid by the producers to the regulator is π, and the total cost for the customers is $(2 + \pi)T$.

Consider now, still in the competitive equilibrium framework, the Business As Usual (BAU) scenario: the demand is met by using coal technology, the price of electricity is 1, the total profit for producers is 0 and the total cost for the customers is T. In this simple example the producers' cost induced by the trading scheme is $T + \pi$; producers must buy more expensive fuel, so a profit T is made by the fuel supplier and the producers have to pay the penalty π. The increase in fuel price, or switching cost, is a marginal cost that must factor into the electricity price. The penalty is a fixed cost paid at the end, but we see that in this trading scheme, this fixed cost is rolled over the entire period and paid by the customers at each time, inducing a windfall profit for the producers. This windfall profit is exactly equal to the market value of the $T - 1$ credits. However, notice that if we increase the demand to $2\,\text{MWh}$ at each time $t = 0$; $1, \ldots, T - 1$ then the windfall profits exceed the market value of the allowances.

Note that Carmona *et al.* define technology by a finite set of production technologies with different cost and emission amounts as compared with our use of a Cobb–Douglas production, with carbon emission defined as an underpriced input of a natural resource. They also assume a finite number of periods up to $T - 1$ for decision making by the producers and fixed demand for electricity not affected by the price that the producers charge.

The model is more general and the options for the producers are more complicated. The production of goods is specified as follows. A finite set I of firms produce and sell a set K of goods at times $0, 1, \ldots, T-1$. Each firm i has access to a set $J_{i,k}$ of different technologies to produce good k that are sources of emissions (e.g. greenhouse gases). Each technology j is characterized by:

- a marginal cost $C_{i,j,k,t}$ of producing one unit of good k at time t;
- a nonnegative emission factor $e_{i,j,k}$ measuring the volume of pollutants emitted per unit of good k produced by firm i with technology j;
- a constant production capacity $K_{i,j,k}$.

For the sake of notation, the following index sets are introduced:

$$M_i = \{(j;k) : k \in K; j \in J_i; k\}, \quad i \in I;$$

$$M = \{(i;j;k) : i \in I; k \in K; j \in J_i; k\}.$$

The main example is the production of electric power. For each time t, firm i produces certain amount of good $k \in K$ throughout the period from 1 to $T - 1$ using the technology j. Since the choice of the production level is based only on present and past observations, the processes for the outputs are also supposed to be adapted. The market is driven by an exogenous and inelastic demand. Denote by D_t^k the demand at time t for good k. For each good $k \in K$, the authors assume that the demand is always smaller than the total production capacity for this good.

As their analysis shows, existence, uniqueness and characterization of some of the equilibrium price processes depend only upon the total number of emission permits issued during the compliance period, not on the way the permits are distributed over time and among the various participating installations. However as the authors demonstrate, the statistical properties of consumer costs and windfall profits depend strongly upon the way permits are allocated. The challenge faced by policy makers is to optimally design these allocation schemes to minimize consumer costs while satisfying emissions reduction targets, controlling producers' windfall profits and setting incentives for the development of cleaner production technologies.

The authors summarize their approach as follows

In the present work, we give a precise mathematical foundation to the analysis of emission trading schemes and quantitatively investigate the impact of emission regulation on consumer costs and firm profits. Based on a model for perfect competition, we show that in equilibrium, a standard emission trading scheme combines two contrasting aspects. On the one hand, the system reduces pollution at the lowest cost for the society, as expected. On the other hand, it forces a notable transfer of wealth from consumers to producers, which in general exceeds the social costs of pollution reduction.

In a perfect economy where all customers are shareholders, windfall profits are redistributed, at least partially through dividends payments. However, this situation is not always the case, and the impact of regulation on prices needs to be addressed. There are several other ways to return part of the windfall profits to the consumers. The most prominent ones are taxation and charging for the initial allowance distribution. Beyond the political risks associated with the levy of new taxes, we will show that one of the main disadvantages of this first method is its poor control of the final level of emissions under random demand for goods and stochastic abatement costs.

One point to note is that the authors consider electricity to be produced in a competitive market where in Sections 9.2 and 9.3, we consider the production of electricity by firms under monopolistic competition. I hope that our brief introduction of the paper in this section may be useful to the readers who may wish to study it more carefully.

9.5.   A Proposal to Regulate CO_2 Emission through a UN Resolution

The problem to regulate CO_2 emission in the world may be different from the problem of regulating pollution in one country. There is the enforcement problem. In the case of air pollution, the national government can be relied upon to ensure that the amount of pollution does not exceed the amount allowed by the number of permits. In the CO_2 emission case, the national government may not be willing to enforce the assigned amount according to the number of permits. If the national governments do not adhere to an international agreement, the CO_2 emission problem is inherently insoluble. We provide a solution under the assumption that the international treaty will be obeyed and offer a formula to decide how to determine (a) the total of CO_2 emission permits and (b) the distribution of these permits.

Scientists and scholars have proposed solutions to the problem of climate change by reducing the rate of CO_2 emission of the entire world. The two components of the problem are the rate at which CO_2 emission should be reduced and the allocation of the amount of reduction or emission among countries. Their opinions differ. For example Pacala and Solocow (2004), Socolow and Pacala (2006) and Socolow and Lam (2007) based their recommendations for the first component on scientific ground. Dyson (2008) on the other hand believes that there is no need to be overly concerned with unduly large amount of CO_2 accumulation in the atmosphere because in the near future "genetically engineered carbon-eating trees" will absorb the excess amount of carbon. He therefore does not recommend regulating the amount of emission. Any proposal by a scientist or scholar to limit carbon emission is irrelevant unless the nations can agree on it. Rather than adding to this list of recommendations I would like to propose a reasonable and democratic process by which the nations can reach a solution of their own on the above two components of the problem, rather than proposing a solution of my own that they should adopt.

Al Gore, former Candidate of the Democratic Party for the Presidency of the United States, received the Nobel Peace Prize 2007 for his contribution to regulate the emission of CO_2 to prevent harmful climate change. The scientific community agrees that if the amount of CO_2 in the atmosphere equals twice the amount that existed before the Industrial Revolution, an intolerable level of global warming will occur. If the rate of carbon emission increases at the rate as it did in the last 30 years, this dangerous level will be reached in about 70 years. Therefore, to slow down the emission of CO_2 is the most urgent task. The task is difficult because people are accustomed to use coal at home for cooking and heating and in factories to generate electricity and to use oil for heating and in driving automobiles. All such use of fossil fuel to generate energy causes the emission of carbon dioxide.

My proposal is based on the following propositions which I hope most citizens and nations in the world can accept.

1. CO_2 emission is affecting the atmosphere, a valuable resource.
2. The atmosphere is collectively owned by the citizens of the world as represented by their national governments, with equal right of ownership to all citizens.

3. Any amount of CO_2 emission in any country has to be paid for by obtaining emission permits.

Based on these propositions a resolution, which consists of the following components, can be proposed to the United Nations.

1. Each member of the United Nations submits a desired amount of total world emission of CO_2 for a given period (of one to three years). The median amount will be adopted.
2. Emission permits are required when carbon is emitted. The number of permits or the total amount of world emission should be distributed equally to the world's citizens under the assumption that each person has an equal right to use the atmosphere in the form of carbon emission.
3. Emission permits, once distributed to the nations, can be bought and sold at mutually agreed upon prices.
4. The government of each country has the responsibility to ensure that the total amount of emission in the country shall not exceed the amount allowed by the permits that it possesses.

To carry out this resolution, nations in the world are required only to vote on the total amount of emission allowed and enforce the amount emitted in their own territory to equal the number of permits that they possess.

The above proposal can be interpreted as a version of "cap and trade" for CO_2 emission permits, except that it includes specific procedures to determine the total amount of emission allowed in the world and the distribution of this amount to all nations.

Some developed countries, such as US, may not be willing to limit its per-capita emission to the world average. Under this proposal, it needs to purchase permits from the world market, which it can afford. The proposal only stipulates that US citizens are entitled to the same number of emission permits or to the use of the same amount of the world atmosphere as other world citizens. If they use more, they should pay for it. In doing so, they are subsidizing the less developed countries in the protection of the environment as many are willing to do. This resolution may not be popular in the US, but its citizens should understand that citizens of other countries have equal right to use the atmosphere and that if they wish to use more per person they should pay for it by purchasing emission permits in the world market.

The idea to have a citizen in the US emit an equal amount as the average for world citizens is probably not acceptable by the people of the US and by members of the US Congress. However, my proposal is not about the amount of emission per person in the US but the number of emission permits distributed to the country. If the US does not have sufficient permits, it can easily afford to purchase them in the world market. This is consistent with the notion that the US should support developing countries in the control of global warming. If we believe that citizens of the world are equally entitled to the same amount of natural resources in the atmosphere, a belief that is hard to refute, they should be given the same number of emission permits. Furthermore, to distribute the emission permits according to population size is already unfair to the poor countries that should get more permits per person because they have emitted less in the past. This proposal already forgives the US for past emissions. Understanding the above justifications, US citizens and their representatives in the US Senate should be willing to support this proposal in a treaty.

Less developed countries like China and India will likely support this proposal because their current emission per capita is below world average and they will benefit from selling their permits to other countries. If China presents this proposal to the United Nations and it is adopted, the world will benefit. Even if it does not pass, China and India will not be criticized for emitting an unreasonable amount of carbon.

One possible criticism of this proposal is that it fails to allow for the history of emission in the past. Developed countries presumably have already emitted large amounts of CO_2, much of which remains in the atmosphere. Would this mean that they should emit less today as compared with the less developed countries? This problem can be solved by revising the distribution of total permits in the above proposal to give more permits to lower-income countries. The number given may be proportional to population size divided by the country's per capita income in PPP units. If a country of the same population size has per capita income twice as large as another it would receive only half as many permits.

An opposite argument can be made to allow citizens of rich countries to be given more emission permits per capita because they have contributed to world economic development, including the innovation of new technology that the developing countries can utilize. Doing so would be like subsidizing the rich because they have contributed more to the economic development of the country. This is objectionable in view of the fact that the rich already enjoy the fruits of their past labor and should not be given more because their past labor is helping others in the country or in the world as the case maybe.

The above discussion on the fair distribution of emission permits suggests that it may be difficult for the nations to reach an agreement on this topic. I believe that giving each world citizen an equal right seems more reasonable and has the highest chance of being accepted by the majority of nations. If this is not true, the proposal can be revised to allow the distribution of emission permits to be more or less than the population size and the nations can vote for an alternative distribution formula.

By comparison, a proposal by Pacala and Socolow (2004) has the following components. (1) The amount of pollution is determined by technical calculations — a straight-line path of reduction of annual emission rate with speed based on "wedges" measuring the contributions of different uses of energy. (2) The above amount is distributed in proportion to the number of persons in each country which has per capita emission exceeding a given level. Their scheme is based on CO_2 emission responsibility for each individual person. No matter where she/he lives, each individual whose CO_2 emissions are above a certain level will be held responsible for mitigation. Supposing we require all those with emissions above a threshold to reduce their CO_2 emissions to the threshold in order to achieve a global target, the sum of all the high-emitters' reductions in a country is its total mitigation responsibility. One application of this scheme shows that to cap the global emissions at the level of 30 $GtCO_2$/year in 2030, 1.1 billion people (almost divided evenly among the four major groups of regions) will be held responsible. Our proposal determines the total quantity by voting and distributes that quantity of permits according to ownership right of the atmosphere, rather than the alleged responsibility to reduce emission. Our scheme is based on the idea of ownership of the atmosphere, how much each person owns and accordingly how much permission is allowed according to his property rights.

There are important economic and political issues associated with the use of emission permits for the control of world carbon emission, not only with reference to the specific proposal presented in this section but for the use of emission permits for this problem in general.

From the economic viewpoint, the above proposal may not adequately consider a country's development history into account. Should a developed country that has contributed not only to its own economic growth but also to the economic growth of other countries which have benefited from its products and technological innovations be given more permits per capita, or fewer permits per capita because it has polluted the environment or emitted more carbon in the past? If we consider the trade-off between increasing world output and polluting the world, we need to estimate the cost of carbon emission or pollution per unit of output, which differs from country to country and from case to case.

From the political point of view, it would not be easy for member nations in the General Assembly to agree on the way the permits should be distributed. Perhaps the regulation of world carbon emission should not be settled by a treaty among the G20 or a group of countries. Even if the question is raised in the General Assembly, there are other complicated and related issues that may make a simple resolution different. One such issue is that some developing countries require the developed countries to provide financing and technology, and to take action first before they will act. But developed countries (mainly EU) would prefer their own scheme to control carbon emission. From China's view point, per capita–based emission is not favored. Even though China has low capita emission at present, according to our scenario study, China's per capita emission level is already above global average emission level. If developed countries will follow the Copenhagen EU proposal, China's per capita carbon emission will be above the average of the developed countries by 2030. Then China will need to follow the deep reduction path as the developed countries, even for the lowest emission scenario for China. However, in the future, when its economy is further developed China may be willing to pay for the excess amount by buying permits in the world market.

References

Carmona, Rene, Max Fehr, Juri Hinz and Arnaud Porchet (2011), "Market Design for Trading Schemes," mimeo, Princeton University.

Dyson, Freeman (2008). "The Question of Global Warming." *The New York Review of Books.* 55(10) June 12, 1–7.

Pacala, S. W. and R. H. Socolow (2004). "Stabilization Wedges: Solving the Climate Problem for the Next 50 Years with Current Technologies," *Science* 305(5686), 968–972.

Socolow, R. H. and S. H. Lam (2007). "Good Enough Tools for Global Warming Policy Making," *Philosophical Transaction of the Royal Society* 365, 897–934.

Socolow, R. H. and S. W. Pacala. (2006). "A Plan to Keep Carbon in Check." *Scientific American* 2006, 1–7.

Chapter 10

Environmental Kuznets Curve

10.1. Introduction

Simon Kuznets contributed significantly to the development of national income accounts and to the understanding of economic development in general. One observation he made concerning income inequality is that at an early stage of development, inequality increases with per-capita income and at a later stage it decreases with income. Plotting inequality against per-capita income or against time, one would find the curve first increasing and then decreasing, i.e., an inverted U-shaped curve. On the subject of pollution or of environmental degradation in general, economists have observed that its relation with per-capita income or the stage of economic development also has an inverted U shape, first increasing and later decreasing. This relation is known as the environmental Kuznets Curve (EKC). One of the early contributions to this topic is Grossman and Kruger (1991).

There has been a vast literature on EKC since the publication of Grossman and Kruger (1991). Much of the available literature raises skepticism of the econometric methods used to test the hypothesis of the EKC, as contained in the survey articles of Stern (2004), Dinda (2004) and especially Romero-Avila (2008). There is also much less consensus on the existence of EKC for CO_2 than for the other traditional pollutants such as SO_2 and NO_x. The reason is that compared with those of other pollutants the impacts of CO_2 are indirect, global, and long term. In Section 10.2, I first present a theory of the EKC as formulated by Andreoni and Levison (2001). Section 10.3 considers the problem of testing that theory. Section 10.4 presents a statistical test for the existence of the EKC using data for 132 countries for the period 1992–2004. The test result supports the EKC.

10.2. A Theory to Explain the Relation Between Pollution and Output

I begin with an explanation of the phenomenon of EKC as given by Andreoni and Levinson (2001).

Assume a linear utility function of consumption C and pollution P, i.e., $U = C - zP$. The amount of pollution P is measured in the units to make it equal to consumption C. The parameter z measures the weight given to P relative to the consumption. Second, pollution is assumed to be a function $P = C - C^\alpha E^\beta$. The first C refers to emission, which is defined in the same units as C. The second term is an abatement function showing that the amount of pollution being cleaned up depends on the level of consumption C because it reflects the level of economic development and the amount E spent to clean up. Hence, we can write the utility function as

$$U = C - zP = (1 - z)C + zC^\alpha E^\beta. \tag{10.1}$$

Consider the special case when $z = 1$ so that the utility function becomes

$$U = C^\alpha E^\beta. \tag{10.2}$$

This utility function is very convenient. In elementary economics textbooks, the theory of consumer behavior based on utility maximization is often explained by using this utility function of two consumption goods C and E. Here C is total consumption and E is the amount of effort to clean up the environment that has utility because it leads to a clean environment through the abatement function $C^\alpha E^\beta$ for the amount of pollution being cleaned up.

Now elementary theory of consumer behavior can be used to obtain the solution for C and E. Let income be M and the budget constraint will be $C + E = M$. Maximizing utility with respect to these two variables by differentiating the Lagrangean

$$L = C^\alpha E^\beta - \lambda(M - C - E),$$

yields the optimum consumption and effort for abatement

$$C^* = [\alpha/(\alpha + \beta)]M \quad E^* = [\beta/(\alpha + \beta)]M. \tag{10.3}$$

The demand function for pollution $P = C - C^\alpha E^\beta$ is therefore

$$P = \frac{\alpha}{\alpha + \beta} M - \frac{\alpha^\alpha \beta^\beta}{(\alpha + \beta)^{\alpha+\beta}} M^{\alpha+\beta}. \tag{10.4}$$

The slope of this function is

$$\frac{\alpha}{\alpha + \beta} - \frac{\alpha^\alpha \beta^\beta}{(\alpha + \beta)^{\alpha+\beta-1}} M^{\alpha+\beta-1}.$$

If the abatement technology has increasing returns or if $\alpha + \beta > 1$, the slope is positive for small values of M and negative for large values of M. Equation (10.4) can therefore explain the phenomenon of the EKC, i.e., when income M goes up pollution P first increases and when M increases further pollution will decrease. If $\alpha + \beta = 2$, pollution P is a quadratic equation of income M, with the coefficient of M^2 being negative.

If z in the utility function does not equal 1, maximizing utility subject to the same budget constraint will yield a relation between P and M of an inverted-U shape if and only if the abatement technology has increasing returns to scale $\alpha + \beta > 1$. Intuitively speaking, as income increases, people spend more for abatement and, if there is increasing returns in abatement, it will lead to more abatement and less pollution.

The authors show that for a general utility function $U(C, P)$ that is quasiconcave in C and $-P$ and for C and $-P$ being normal goods, optimal pollution will eventually decline back to zero for some sufficiently large income if the abatement function $A(C, M-C)$ is concave and homogeneous of degree $k > 1$ and if the marginal utility of consumption at zero pollution is not too small as compared with the marginal disutility of pollution evaluated at zero pollution.

10.3. Statistical Testing of the Andreoni–Levinson EKC

If data on pollution P and income M are available, we can use nonlinear regression to estimate Equation (10.4)

$$P = \frac{\alpha}{\alpha + \beta} M - \frac{\alpha^\alpha \beta^\beta}{(\alpha + \beta)^{\alpha+\beta}} M^{\alpha+\beta}. \tag{10.5}$$

Nonlinear regression can be used to estimate the parameters α and β.

In the special case when $\alpha + \beta$ equals 2, P becomes a quadratic equation in income M. But the Equation (10.5) imposes two restrictions on its parameters: First, the intercept is zero. Second, the coefficient of the term $M^{\alpha+\beta}$ is negative while the coefficient of the linear term is positive. These restrictions can be tested under the null hypothesis that the theory as specified by Equation (10.5) is correct.

For the more general case with z not equal to 1, it can easily be shown that the theory implies the following consumption function

$$C^* = \frac{\alpha}{\alpha + \beta} M + \frac{1 - z}{z(\alpha + \beta)C^{\alpha-1}(M - C)^{\beta-1}}. \qquad (10.6)$$

The theory also has an abatement function $A = C^{\alpha}E^{\beta}$ to be estimated. The parameters α and β estimated from this abatement function have to be consistent with those estimated from the consumption function. While the theory of Andreoni and Levinson is attractive in deriving an inverted-U shape for the relation between pollution P and income M, the consumption function, function for expenditure E on abatement and the abatement function may not fit the data. For the purpose of testing the hypothesis of the EKC, a formulation without the specific restrictions by the theory of Andreoni and Levinson (2001) would be more useful. I will pursue the testing of one version of the EKC in the next section.

10.4.   Statistical Testing of One Version of the EKC

The theory presented in Section 10.2 illustrates that it is possible to provide a simple theory to explain an EKC. For the purpose of statistical testing the existence of the phenomenon of the EKC, a specific model is used. This section reports the result of testing the existence of the EKC using this model. The hypothesis is that the relation between pollution y and income x is quadratic and that the coefficient of the quadratic term is negative. Equation (10.5) imposes restrictions of zero intercept term and on the relation between the coefficient of the first term, income M, and the coefficient of the second term, $M^{\alpha+\beta}$. Because there is much debate in the literature on the existence of the EKC, we do not assume the specific formulation of Equation (10.5) by Andreoni and Levinson (2001). To avoid the numerous econometric problems arising from using panel data regression for this test as discussed in Chapter 7, the t-test of Ibragimov and Müller (2010) employed in Chapter 7 is used.

For the purpose of this section, an EKC is defined as an empirical relationship during the course of economic development that per-capita CO_2 emissions first increased with per-capita real GDP and later decreased with per-capita real GDP. This definition is accepted in much of the literature, e.g. Stern (2004), Dinda (2004) and Romero-Avila (2008), although disagreement on definition exists. We will test only the above formulation in this section.

Specifically our formulation of the EKC is stated in the following regression:

$$Y_{it} = \alpha_i + \beta x_{it} + \gamma x_{it}^2 + u_{it}. \tag{10.7}$$

In this equation Y_{it} denotes the natural log of CO_2 emissions from energy use per capita of country i in year t; x_{it} denotes the natural log of real GDP per capita of country i in year t and u_{it} is a random residual which may be heteroskedastic, correlated among countries and serially correlated. We are interested in testing the null hypothesis that the coefficient γ is zero against the alternative hypothesis that it is negative, given data available for $i = 0, 1, 2, \ldots, n$ and $t = 1, 2, \ldots, T$.

I treat the econometric hypothesis for the EKC stated in (10.7) as generated by a model that is valid historically only during the sample period. Others may treat EKC as a hypothesis for economic development of different countries, which will continue to hold in the future, after the sample period. This is an important limitation of the test of this section. Here I only advance the hypothesis that the data for different countries during the historical sample period are generated by a stochastic model valid for this period only. In the future, the EKC relationship may change for various reasons related to institutional and technological changes but such possible changes are beyond the scope of the present discussion. Furthermore, there are other statistical formulations with different measures of environmental degradation for the dependent variable. These formulations can be interesting but my attention here is restricted only to the formulation as stated in Equation (10.7). I note that this method to test the EKC hypothesis applies to other formulations as well, including those using other measures of environmental degradation.

The statistical test employed for the null hypothesis that the coefficient γ in Equation (10.7) is zero against the alternative hypothesis that it is negative is a simple t-test performed as follows. Assume that we have data on all variables for $i = 1, 2, \ldots, n$ and $t = 1, 2, \ldots, T$. For each year t, we perform a regression to estimate (10.7) using data for the n countries and obtain an estimate c_t of γ for $t = 1, \ldots, T$. We then use a t statistic to test the null hypothesis that $c_t(t = 1, 2, \ldots, T)$ come from a population with mean $\gamma = 0$ against the alternative hypothesis that the mean is negative. This test is valid provided that the c_t for different t are statistically independent or nearly so. The test is based on Ibragimov and Müller (2010).

International data for CO_2 emissions and GDP per capita in PPP are used. The CO_2 data are from *CO_2 Emissions from Fuel Combustion* Vol. 2007 of International Energy Agency (IEA). The GDP per-capita data are from World Development Indicators (WDI) 2006 of the World Bank. The panel data we use cover the years 1992–2004 and 132 countries for each year.[a]

To construct a Student's t-test for EKC, we perform cross-section regressions based on (10.7) using these data as reported in Table 10.1. The estimates of the coefficient γ of x^2 for these 13 years are, respectively, $-0.176 \, (-2.89)$, $-0.157 \, (-2.55)$, $-0.142 \, (-2.38)$, $-1.42 \, (-2.35)$, $-0.111 \, (-1.79)$, $-125 \, (-2.16)$, $-0.139 \, (-2.51)$, -1.39 (-2.56), $-0.145 \, (-2.83)$, $-1.38 \, (-2.67)$, $-1.33 \, (-2.62)$, -0.094 (-1.61), and $-0.110 \, (-2.10)$. The number in parenthesis after each estimated coefficient is its t statistic but these t statistics are not used in our test at all since t tests based on them can be subject to econometric problems if the residuals for different countries are correlated. We only compute a t statistic using these 13 point estimates and obtain a value of -22.16383. The evidence is extremely strong for supporting the alternative hypothesis that the coefficient

---

[a]I acknowledge with thanks the able assistance from Jie Li in conducting the empirical analysis of this section.

Table 10.1.   Cross-section EKC regressions for years 1992–2004.

Year	α	β	γ	R^2	Root MSE
1992	-22.1 (-4.95)	4.21 (4.01)	-0.176 (-2.89)	0.6706	0.941
1993	-20.7 (-4.51)	3.89 (3.63)	-0.158 (-2.55)	0.6734	0.933
1994	-19.6 (-4.40)	3.62 (3.49)	-0.142 (-2.38)	0.6754	0.932
1995	-19.3 (-4.23)	3.59 (3.39)	-0.142 (-2.35)	0.6894	0.884
1996	-17.0 (-3.62)	3.05 (2.81)	-0.111 (-1.79)	0.6905	0.870
1997	-18.1 (-4.11)	3.29 (3.24)	-0.126 (-2.16)	0.7005	0.850
1998	-19.1 (-4.51)	3.54 (3.63)	-0.140 (-2.51)	0.7118	0.829
1999	-19.1 (-4.56)	3.53 (3.68)	-0.140 (-2.56)	0.7210	0.808
2000	-19.5 (-5.00)	3.63 (4.03)	-0.145 (-2.83)	0.7279	0.797
2001	-19.0 (-4.79)	3.51 (3.85)	-0.138 (-2.67)	0.7255	0.796
2002	-18.7 (-4.80)	3.43 (3.82)	-0.133 (-2.62)	0.7332	0.782
2003	-15.8 (-3.47)	2.75 (2.65)	-0.094 (-1.61)	0.7290	0.787
2004	-17.1 (-4.19)	3.04 (3.27)	-0.110 (-2.10)	0.7362	0.773

is negative in the population. Thus our formulation of the EKC as given in Equation (10.7) is strongly confirmed.

Here I briefly comment on several critical evaluations of the evidence supporting the EKC. First, Romero-Avila (2008) presents three sets of problems in using panel cointegration techniques to estimate an EKC. First, the different orders of integration in the dependent variable CO_2 per capita and the independent variable real GDP per capita for the world as a whole and for Asian and African countries in particular make the use of panel cointegration techniques invalid. Second, the data may contain multiple structural breaks. Third, there is cross-sectional dependence in the regression residuals. As pointed out earlier, since I am not using panel cointegration methods to estimate Equation (10.7) all three criticisms do not apply to our t test.

Dinda (2004) surveys both the theoretical justifications and empirical evidence for the EKC. This section is not concerned with the former. Regarding the latter, Dinda points out that there is no agreement in the literature on the income level at which environmental degradation starts declining. Although this income level is not the main concern of the test of this section the regressions presented in Table 10.1 show that for the period 1992 to 2004 the coefficients of income per capita and of its square are quite similar for these years. This implies that the first derivatives of the regressions are similar. When the first derivatives are set equal to zero, the value of income per capita is not too different in these years and provide an estimate of the level at which the EKC begins to decline. The evidence presented in this section applies only for the period 1992–2004 and may not be valid in other periods.

Stern (2004) points out that because developing countries are addressing environmental issues, they may not have to go through a period of deteriorating environmental standards as the EKC implies. This proposition may be valid for the future but it does not invalidate the statistical support presented in this section for the EKC for the period 1992–2004.

10.5. Summary

This chapter begins with an exposition of a theory of the EKC provided by Adreoni and Levinson (2001). After briefly discussing statistical testing of that specific theory, attention is given to a formulation of the EKC without specific restrictions given by Andreoni and Levinson (2001) because there has been much debate in the literature of environmental economics on the existence of the EKC. The empirical part of this chapter has concentrated on this formulation and treats EKC purely as an empirical hypothesis without using a specific theoretical model for its derivation. A simple t-test is applied, which is based only on the cross-section estimates of the 13 coefficients of the square of log (GDP per capita) in the regressions of log(emission of CO_2 per capita) for 132 countries and the 13 years from 1992 to 2004. The result conclusively confirms that this coefficient is negative, thus providing a very strong support of this hypothesis during the period observed. I have also pointed out that several critical evaluations of the evidence supporting the EKC in the literature do not apply to the test being reported.

References

Andreoni, James and Arik Levinson (2001). "The Simple Analytics of the Environmental Kuznets Curve," *Journal of Public Economics*, 80, 269–286.

Bin-bin, Jiang "Demand for Coal v. Natural Gas in Guangzhou, Shanghai" in *Stanford U Series*.

Dinda, Soumyananda (2004). "Environmental Kuznets Curve Hypothesis: A Survey." *Ecological Economics*, 49, 431–455.

Grossman, G. M. and A. B. Krueger (1995). "Economic Growth and the Environment." *Quarterly Journal of Economics*, 110, 353–377.

Ibragimov, Rustam and Ulrich K. Müller (2010). "*t*-Statistic Based Correlation and Heterogeneity Robust Inference." *Journal of Business & Economic Statistics*, 28(4), 453–468.

Perron, P. (1989). "The Great Crash, the Oil Price Shock, and the Unit Root Hypothesis." *Econometrica*, 57(6), 1361–1401.

Romero-Avila, Diego (2008). "Questioning the Empirical Basis of the Environmental Kuznets Curve for CO_2: New Evidence from a Panel Stationary Test Robust to Multiple Breaks and Cross-Dependence." *Ecological Economics*, 559–574.

Stern, David I. (2004). "The Rise and Fall of the Environmental Kuznets Curve." *World Development*, 32(8), 1419–1439.

Chapter 11

Clean Energy and International Efforts to Solve Environmental Problems

11.1. Introduction

The use of clean energy, meaning the use of energy without emission of harmful pollutants, can be achieved in three ways. First, current technology can be used to reduce the amount of pollutants emitted to the atmosphere from the use of energy sources such as coal and oil. Second, new technology can be adopted to reduce the amount of harmful emission per unit of output from a given energy source. Third, energy sources other than oil or coal can be exploited, which include natural gas, solar energy, wind, hydroelectricity and nuclear fusion. These are the topics of Sections 2, 3 and 4. Practical problems in introducing clean energy in the United States and the role of business enterprises in promoting clean energy will be discussed in Sections 5 and 6. Sections 7 and 8 deal with China's effort to promote the use and development of clean energy and possible US-China cooperation in promoting clean energy technology. Finally possible roles of the United Nations in coordinating international efforts to reduce CO_2 emission are set forth in Section 9.

11.2. Reducing the Emission of Pollutants from a Given Energy Source

11.2.1. SO_2 Scrubbers

Given the amount of SO_2 generated by power plants, SO_2 scrubbers can be used to reduce the amount of carbon emitted to the atmosphere.

As an example, the control of air pollution by the use of SO_2 scrubbers in China was reported in XU Yuan (2011a and 2011b). In the 10th Five-Year Plan (2001–2005), China's SO_2 emissions went up by 28% and were nowhere close to meeting the goal of reducing emissions by 10%. However, in the 11th Five-Year Plan (2006–2010), the trend was reversed. In 2008, China achieved a 9% reduction of SO_2 emissions from the 2005 level, almost reaching the goal of a 10% reduction by 2010. China managed to install SO_2 scrubbers at both old and newly built coal power plants. At the end of 2008, China had 363 GW_e of SO_2 scrubbers, or 60% of the total capacity of coal power generation (601 GW_e). By comparison, the ratio at the end of 2005 was only 10%.

This achievement came from the central government's effort in mobilizing both the leaders of local governments and managers of coal power plants. For the former, two measures were taken in the 11th Five-Year Plan: (1) promotion and removal of leaders according to the success in the operation of SO_2 scrubbers. (2) suspension of construction of large projects which may affect the environment (including new coal power plants over 200 MW_e) since by law large construction projects require ratification by the Ministry of Environmental Protection based on an assessment of the environmental impact of the project. To increase the capacity of supervision by means of site visits, the total personnel at all government levels increased from 37,934 in 2001 to 52,845 in 2006, or by 39.3%.

In providing incentives to managers of power plants, the most important policy in the 11th Five-Year Plan for the operation of SO_2 scrubbers is called "desulfurized electricity price premium": After installing an SO_2 scrubber, a coal power plant is allowed to sell its electricity to the electric grid at a price 15 RMB/MWh higher than the original price if the SO_2 scrubber is under normal operation, whereas it would be fined 75 RMB/MWh if its SO_2 scrubber were shut down. Although many coal power plants with SO_2 scrubbers have been receiving the price premium from as early as 2004, the penalty and other detailed regulations were not enforced until July 2007.

11.2.2. *Carbon Capture and Storage (CCS)*

As the term CCS suggests, technology is available to capture the carbon emitted from using fossil fuels, and to store it underground. However, problems arise in finding the space underground to store the captured carbon and in the leakage of carbon over the course of time. Technological improvement is required for CCS to be successfully adopted.

There are different strategies for storing emitted carbon. Carbon waste can securely be stored underground, either near the location of energy generation or after being shipped to locations not far from the place of origin. Alternatively, carbon waste can be orbited in space.

There is much disagreement on the efficacy of CCS, including the safety of carbon storage underground or in space. Experts do not know the size of the geological repositories and how much leakage there might be. The disagreement may be reduced in future, when the technology for CCS improves.

11.3. New Technology to Reduce Emission

11.3.1. *New Coal Power Plants*

New and less polluting coal power plants are available but the replacement of old and more polluting power plants is costly and time consuming. Since a large number of new power plants were needed in China, most of them were built with the new technology and are less polluting.

According to an article in the *New York Times* on May 10, 2009, China had emerged in the previous two years as the world's leading builder of more efficient, less polluting coal power plants, mastering the technology and driving down the cost. China's investment in cleaner plants will reduce emissions of dirty gases and other chemical pollutants, improve air quality, and encourage more measures in other fields of manufacturing and production to better protect the environment. The policies established by the Chinese government and supported by the public owed much to the 2008 Summer Olympic Games in Beijing. While the United States was still debating whether to build more efficient coal-fired power plants that use extremely hot steam, China began building such plants at a rate of one a month.

The *New York Times* report said that construction had stalled in the United States on a new generation of low-pollution power plants that turn coal into a gas before burning it, although the Obama administration might have revived one such plant. China had already approved equipment purchases for one such power plant, to be assembled in suburban Tianjin. China has begun requiring power companies to retire an older, more polluting power plant for each new plant they build. On the other hand, Western countries continue to rely on coal-fired power plants built decades ago, with outdated and inefficient technology that consumes a lot of coal and emits considerable amounts of CO_2 per unit of energy generated.

However, China's coal-fired power sector still has many problems, and greenhouse gas emissions from the country are expected to continue to increase. China's aim is to use the newest technologies to limit the rate of increase. As of 2009, only half the country's coal-fired power plants had the equipment to filter out the sulfur compounds that cause acid rain from their emissions. Among China's newly built plants, not all are modern. Only about 60 percent of the new plants are being built using newer technology that is highly efficient, but more expensive. The least efficient plants in China today convert 27 to 36 percent of the energy in coal into electricity. The most efficient plants achieve an efficiency as high as 44 percent, meaning they can cut global warming emissions by more than a third compared with the weakest plants. In the United States, the most efficient plants achieve around 40 percent efficiency, because they do not use the highest steam temperatures being used in China. The average efficiency of American coal-fired plants is still higher than the average efficiency of Chinese power plants because China built so many inefficient plants over the past decade. But China is rapidly closing the gap by using some of the world's most advanced designs. As of November 2012, there were 620 new coal-fired plants operating in China and the government was planning to add about 160 more within four years.

11.3.2. *Light Emitting Diodes (LEDs)*

Light emitting diodes or LEDs are an emerging lighting technology. The new lights last more than 22 years and reduce energy consumption and CO_2 emissions enormously. Studies suggest that a complete conversion to LEDs could decrease CO_2 emissions from electric power use for lighting by up to 50 percent in just over 20 years. In the United States, lighting accounts for about 6 percent of all energy use. Conversion to LED lighting is potentially the most cost effective of a number of simple approaches to tackling global warming using existing technology.

LEDs are more than twice as efficient as compact fluorescent bulbs, currently the standard for greener lighting. Unlike compact fluorescents, LEDs turn on quickly and are compatible with dimmer switches. While fluorescent bulbs contain mercury, which requires special disposal, LED bulbs contain no toxic elements, and last so long that disposal is not much of an issue. In the US, General Electric and Philips have begun making LEDs. The manufacture of LEDs is increasing rapidly around the world. Demand for this product around the world is increasing although the cost is high — it takes five or more years to recoup losses through electricity savings.

11.3.3. *Catalysts for Supersonic Airplane Engine Fuel*

A team at Princeton University's School of Engineering and Applied Science has been studying how fuel additives made of tiny particles known as nanocatalysts can help supersonic jets fly faster and make diesel engines cleaner and more efficient. Composed of snippets of sheets of carbon that are only a single atom thick, the particles have been shown to help fuels ignite and burn faster. This technology may be applied in the next generation of combustion engines. This is an example of using technology to improve the efficiency of a given energy source, reducing pollution and fuel use at the same time.

11.4. Alternative Sources of Energy

11.4.1. *Natural Gas*

Although natural gas is a fossil fuel, its use does not lead to carbon emission as the use of coal and oil does. There is much disagreement on the amount of natural gas that can be profitably extracted in the United States.

According to an article in the *New York Times* dated June 26, 2011, data for more than 10,000 wells in three major shale gas formations raise questions about the industry's prospects. There is a vast amount of gas in those formations but the question is how affordably the gas can be extracted. The amount of gas produced by many of the successful wells is falling much faster than initially predicted by energy companies, making it more difficult for them to turn a profit over the long run. Federal and state lawmakers are considering the increase in subsidies for the natural gas business in the hope that it will provide low-cost energy for decades to come. But if natural gas ultimately proves more expensive to extract from the ground than has been predicted, investment in extracting it may not be profitable and consumers will pay a higher price for electricity and home heating. On the other hand, shale gas will become more economically attractive as the price of gas rises, technology evolves and demand for gas grows, possibly with help from federal subsidies. Much disagreement and uncertainty remain concerning the cost and profitability of developing shale gas as a source of energy.

11.4.2. *Solar Energy*

Much progress has been made in generating electricity with solar panels. Solar energy can also produce hydrogen which can be used to make batteries to propel cars. The major limit to the use of solar panels at present is that for most applications its cost is higher than that of conventional fuels. It also requires a large amount of sunlight. Hence in areas with plenty of sunlight such as Inner Mongolia, solar power is being used.

Solar photovoltaic (PV) panels convert power from the sun to electricity or to hydrogen. There are two main types of PV panels, produced by the conventional crystalline silicon technology and by thin film technology. Solar PV is still expensive and its application still in its infancy. Government subsidies are required to encourage production and technological innovation.

Because of the large potential demand for solar energy across the world, many corporations are producing and developing solar PV panels. In recent years, production of solar panels increased rapidly in China, mainly as a result of government subsidies. Production declined as demand from Europe was reduced as a result of world recession. In Europe, Germany is known to be the leader in the development of solar energy, but the cost effectiveness of the government effort is subject to question.

11.4.3. Wind

The problems plaguing the development of wind farms are similar to those of other forms of alternative energy: how to reduce the cost by applying more up-to-date technology in production and how the farms can be made more environmentally friendly by inventing new technology. One new technology that provides an energy efficient way to convert wind energy to electric energy is to have the propellers facing upwards rather than facing the direction of the wind, so that the axles below will rotate in the same direction that is required to generate mechanical energy.

Governments can provide economic incentives to promote the use of existing technology which is more up-to-date and efficient. For example, in China the Renewable Energy Law of 2005 provides favorable tax status for alternative energy investments and has promoted the development of renewable energy, especially wind. While wind-generated energy currently accounts for only 0.4 percent of China's total electricity supply, China is rapidly becoming the world's fastest growing market for wind power, trailing behind only the US, Germany and Spain in the capacity of existing wind farms. It had doubled its total wind energy capacity in the four years ending 2010, and passed the United States in 2011 as the world's largest market for wind power equipment. Wind energy in China has a potential to provide as much as 24.7 petawatt-hours of electricity supply annually — more than seven times China's current consumption.

11.4.4. Hydroelectricity

Dams harness energy from the flow of water. The Three Gorges Dam in China generates electric power and controls flooding, but required people to be moved from their homes. Another well-known problem is that the accumulation of sand at the bottom of the dam affects the natural environment and needs to be cleaned up regularly. Many people have debated whether it was a correct decision for the Chinese government to build this dam although it is now providing electricity to a large part of the Chinese population.

11.4.5. *Fusion*

Fusion power refers to power generated by nuclear fusion reactions. In this kind of reaction, two light atomic nuclei fuse to form a heavier nucleus and, in doing so, release energy. In a more general sense, the term can also refer to the production of net usable power from a fusion source. China is building considerably more nuclear power plants than the rest of the world combined, and these do not emit CO_2 after they are built. Fusion is the largest source of energy but there may be problems in storing safely the waste products.

The safety problem with using nuclear power plants is well-illustrated by the disaster at the Fukushima Daiichi reactors in northeastern Japan in March 2011, as well as the flooding of the Missouri River in Nebraska in June 2011. Flooding is always a potential risk for nuclear reactors, as nuclear reactors require electric power to pump water to cool the structures even when they are shut down. Without the cooling power, dangerous nuclear radiation can leak out and cause harm to the nearby population.

11.4.6. *Biofuels*

Biofuels can be generated by perennial plants, crop residuals, wood and forest residues, crops, algae and even industrial wastes. The major consideration in using biofuels include the cost of production and the possible negative impact on the environment. For instance, growing corn produces a significant amount of greenhouse gases through the use of fertilizers and tractor fuel, and processing corn into ethanol requires fuel to be burned for heat. Much research is being conducted to solve these problms and to make the production of biofuels economical and environmentally friendly.

An important area of research is on algae as a source of biofuels. For example the Solix Biofuels plant of the Southern Ute Indian Reservation in southwest Colorado is conducting promising experiments in this direction based on the fact that algae can absorb CO_2 in the water. Many other companies are also trying to find a cost-effective way to turn algae into fuel that can be used in a regular diesel engine. Solix's project facility is next to the natural gas processing plant for access to the CO_2 waste stream, which will be used to nourish the algae. This allows CO_2 from the processing of natural gas to be recycled, so that the net amount of CO_2 discharged will be reduced even though the burning of biofuels will discharge some CO_2.

11.4.7. *Use of Electricity to Replace Gasoline for Automobiles*

To reduce the emission of CO_2 from using oil as autotmobile fuel, an increasing number of automobiles are being powered by electricity. The use of electricity is more environmentally friendly as it reduces CO_2 emissions, although the generation of electricity may itself adversely affect the environment to some extent. Consumers are buying automobiles fueled by electricity not only because these automobiles emit less CO_2, but also because they are more economical to run.

In the following sections I will discuss some possible developments in the adoption of clean energy.

11.5. Practical Problems in the US in Defining Renewable Energy

Since the use of renewable energy enables the user to receive tax subsidies and other economic benefits from the US government, many industrial users are trying to broaden the definition of renewable energy in order to receive these benefits. On May 25, 2009, the *New York Times* carried an article to describe this phenomenon.

> In some states, the definition of "renewable" or "alternative" has already expanded. In Pennsylvania, waste coal and methane from coal mines receive the same treatment

as solar panels and wind turbines. In Nevada, old tires can count as a renewable fuel, provided microwaves are used to break down their chemical structure.

About half of the 28 states with renewable mandates include electricity generated by burning garbage (the District of Columbia also has a quota for renewable energy). In Florida, the nuclear power industry is lobbying to be included but has not yet succeeded.

Among states that have already adopted quotas for renewable energy, the standards vary from Wisconsin's, which requires that 10 percent of all power come from renewable sources by 2015, to those of Oregon and Minnesota, which call for 25 percent from renewable sources by 2025. California is raising its mandate to 33 percent by 2020, though its utilities have already indicated that the existing quota — 20 percent by 2010 — will be difficult to meet.

In some states, quotas for renewable energy are paired with mandates for advanced technologies that are not necessarily renewable. For example, Ohio, which currently receives nearly two-thirds of its electricity from burning coal, requires that 25 percent of the state's electricity must come from renewable or advanced technologies by 2025, but of that, half must come from core renewable sources, and some of the remainder can come from burning chemically treated coal.

This case illustrates a phenomenon — when the government offers incentives to encourage certain desirable behavior, the affected parties will find ways to reap the benefits while circumventing the rule of the government.

11.6. Role of Business Enterprises in Promoting Clean Energy

Efforts of business enterprises to promote the use and development of clean energy was discussed in the World Business Summit on Climate Change held on May 24, 2009, in Copenhagen.

According to the report "Green Jobs and Clean Energy Economy" issued by the Copenhagen Climate Council, the exploitation and use of low-carbon clean energy can create business opportunities, bringing with them millions of employment opportunities. The report suggested that if international communities adopt appropriate energy policies to encourage large-scale strategic investment in clean energy, it would not only be conducive to improving the environment, but could bring a large number of job opportunities and create economic growth.

However, after the financial crisis that began in 2008, many enterprises lack capital and time to pursue the goal of becoming clean energy oriented businesses. In order to dispel the enterprises' worries, relevant research institutions released analytical reports at the above mentioned meeting, pointing out that the cost of dealing with climate change is small.

Two main objectives for enterprises are to generate profit for the shareholders and to fulfill their social responsibilities. To reduce harmful emissions during operations and to develop clean energy are part of their social responsibilities. Today major enterprises all over the world are fulfilling these social responsibilities while their profits can satisfy their shareholders at the same time.

11.7. China's Effort to Promote the Use and Development of Clean Energy

In the 11th Five-Year Plan, China decided to greatly increase the production of biomass energy, the supply of electricity from burning of municipal solid waste and agricultural waste, and the production of solid biomass fuels, bio-ethanol and bio-diesel. The 11th Five-Year Plan included targets to achieve 5 million kW of grid inter-connected wind power and 5.5 million kW of grid inter-connected electricity from biomass combustion.

Current efforts to offset coal consumption include developing natural gas and coal-bed methane infrastructure, increasing the number of combined heat and power plants, adding approximately 3,000 megawatts (MW) of hydropower annually, and developing renewable energy resources such as wind and photovoltaics for electricity generation. For China's electricity generation, renewable sources of energy (including hydroelectricity) accounted for 18.6 percent in 2001, second to coal. With assistance from the United Nations and the United States, China hopes to embark on a multi-million dollar renewable energy strategy to combat pollution.

China has established a National Working Group for Dealing with Climate Change since 1990, and in 2007 the group became the National Leading Group for Dealing with Climate Change, directed by the Premier. This group has been devoted to fostering the Clean Development Mechanism (CDM), which specially emphasizes the utilization of renewable energy under an emission trade framework.

China has made a great effort to develop hydropower. The construction of The Three Gorges Dam was started in 1994 and the dam became fully operational around 2011. It is the world's largest hydroelectric power station. According to BP Statistical Review — Full Report 2009, the annual hydroelectric energy produced in China in 2008 was 585.2TWh. (The problem of using hydropower was discussed in Section 11.4.4.)

According to China's National Climate Change Program, China is also promoting the development of bio-energy. There are more than 17 million household biogas digesters, that generate 6,500 million cubic meters of biogas annually. The installed capacity of biomass generation is about 2 GW, among which sugar-cane fired power capacity is about 1.7 GW.

Western countries continue to rely heavily on coal-fired power plants built decades ago with outdated, inefficient technology that burn a lot of coal and emit considerable amounts of CO_2. China, on the other hand, has begun requiring power companies to retire an older, more polluting power plant for each new plant they build.

China's coal-fired power sector still has many problems, and emissions of greenhouse gases from the country are expected to continue increasing. China is intending to use the newest technologies to limit the rate of increase. Only half the country's coal-fired power plants have the equipment to filter out sulfur compounds that cause acid rain from their emissions, and even power plants with that technology do not always use it. China has not begun regulating some of the emissions that lead to heavy smog in big cities. Even among China's newly built plants, only about 60 percent use newer technology that is highly efficient but more expensive.

An efficient power plant burns less coal and emits less CO_2 for each unit of electricity it generates. Experts say the least efficient plants in China today convert 27 to 36 percent of the energy in coal into electricity. The most efficient plants achieve an efficiency as high as 44 percent, meaning they can cut global warming emissions by more than a third compared with the weakest plants. In the United States, the most efficient plants achieve around 40 percent efficiency, because they do not use the highest steam temperatures being used in China. The average efficiency of American coal-fired plants is still higher than the average efficiency of Chinese power plants, because China built so many inefficient plants over the past decade. But China is rapidly closing the gap by using some of the world's most advanced designs. Technology is available to create power plants that contribute virtually nothing to global warming. Many countries hope to develop such plants, though progress has been slow.

China has been making other efforts to reduce its greenhouse gas emissions. It managed to double its total wind energy capacity in each of the four years up to 2011. However, after China set out an ambitious plan in 2011 to build 5,000 megawatts of offshore wind turbines in four years, enough to power 5.4 million homes, less than 10 percent of that capacity was completed in 2014. Officials said that the goal could not be met because of technical difficulties in installing wind turbines in designated coastal locations. The slow pace in China was matched by the US, which had no offshore wind farms after more than a decade of development efforts. In Europe, the only continent with any significant sea-based wind power, companies have scrapped plans for more than 5,700 megawatts since November 2013.

Coal remains the cheapest energy source in China by a wide margin. China has the world's third largest coal reserve, after the United States and Russia. Coal will remain the dominant power source in China for some time to come. By adopting "ultra-supercritical" technology, which uses extremely hot steam to achieve the highest possible efficiency, and by building many identical power plants at the same time, China has cut costs dramatically through economies of scale. It can now cost a third less to build an ultra-supercritical power plant in China than to build a less efficient coal-fired plant in the United States. China has become the world's leading builder of more efficient, less polluting coal power plants, mastering the technology and driving down the cost. While the United States was still debating whether to build more efficient coal-fired power plants that use extremely hot steam, China was building such plants at a rate of one a month.

11.8.   Possible US-China Cooperation in Promoting Clean Energy Technology

In January 2008 the US sent a clean-energy trade mission to China and India to support President George W. Bush's international framework on climate change, energy security, and economic growth, which was first announced on May 31, 2007. The so-called Major Economies Process (MEP) involves 15 major economies and the Asia-Pacific Partnership (APP) on Clean Development and Climate.

The first meeting of the MEP was held in Washington, DC on September 27, 2007. Its purpose was to get the world's largest energy users and largest producers of greenhouse gases, in both developed and developing nations, to establish a new international approach to climate change in 2008 and, ultimately, create a global agreement by 2009 under the United Nations Framework Convention on Climate Change.

The APP is a public–private sector partnership comprising seven partner countries: Australia, Canada, China, India, Japan, South Korea, and the United States. Those countries represent half of the world's economy, population, and energy consumption. They work together to break down policy barriers and to facilitate commercial deployment of technologies that reduce greenhouse gas emissions and enhance energy security.

Within this framework, former US Commerce Assistant Secretary David Bohigian led the Second Clean-Energy Trade Mission to China in September 2008. The mission consisted of 17 US companies with advanced technology ranging from solar power to clean coal. Bohigian set forth plans for Sino-US collaboration on developing clean energy technology. The two countries were expected to work together in the development of alternative energy. The US clean-energy companies were to help China meet its enormous energy demands while deploying technology that would benefit the environment and yield benefits to the companies. As of 5 April 2011, the APP concluded its joint work. A number of individual projects were expected to continue. In the five years of its existence, the APP enhanced partnerships between the public and private sectors and deepened cooperation among its seven partner countries. Since the APP's 2006 launch, a number of partnerships have emerged which are undertaking public--private cooperation involving APP countries and other partners.

11.9. Possible Role of the United Nations in Coordinating International Efforts to Reduce CO_2 Emission

Possible international efforts to control carbon emissions are contained in a report, United Nations (2014), prepared for the UN Secretary General and issued on Tuesday, July 8, 2014. This report prescribes specific actions for the world's biggest economies to prevent catastrophic climate change. It explores the technological paths available for the world's 15 main economies to maintain reasonable rates of growth and at the same time cut their carbon emissions enough by 2050 to prevent intolerable climatic change. The study was to help to build momentum for a UN climate change summit in New York in September 2014 and to advance negotiations in order to reach a global climate deal by the end of 2015.

The study looks at the world's 15 biggest economies: America, Australia, Brazil, Britain, Canada, China, France, Germany, India, Indonesia, Japan, Mexico, Russia, South Africa, and South Korea, which between them account for 70% of global emissions. It answers three important questions. First, what is the objective of preventing global climate change? Second, what is needed to achieve this objective, in terms of the amount of carbon emission allowed? Third, what kinds of technology and what kinds of international cooperation are required to achieve this objective?

The objective is to keep the atmosphere from warming more than 2 degrees Celsius, or 3.6 degrees Fahrenheit, above the preindustrial average of the late 19th century. Most of the countries in the world have already committed to this target in 2009 at the climate summit meeting in Copenhagen. To achieve this objective, CO_2 emissions from energy use in industrial production and human consumption would have to fall to at most 1.6 tons a year per person on the planet by midcentury. This amount is less than a tenth of annual American emissions per person today and less than a third of the world average. To reduce the use of energy to this extent will require significant changes in the way energy is used, development of new technologies for energy production as well as appropriate international cooperation.

Concerning the kinds of technology available, carbon capture and storage (CCS) is supposed to be available in about 10 years. Second generation biofuels are expected to come into play by 2020. Hydrogen fuel cells and power storage technology are to be deployed starting around 2030. These technologies all exist today and are available for use although adopting them will take time and is costly.

Concerning the kinds of technology required, different countries offer different solutions. The American team built several paths that would hit the target, using different mixes of nuclear power, renewable energy and fossil fuels with CCS technology. So did the Russian team, aided by the expected shrinking of the Russian population. But the Chinese team recognized the country's vast heavy industry — its steel makers and cement plants, which use enormous amounts of energy. The best China could do was chart a path that took CO_2 emissions to some 3.4 tons per person by midcentury. Overall, the teams built plausible technological paths to cut annual emissions across the 15 countries only to about 2.3 tons per person, above the target of 1.6 tons per person. The kind of technological changes required to reduce CO_2 sufficiently is discussed in Barrett (2009).

Concerning the cooperation of nations, the report insists that every country, rich and poor, must reduce annual CO_2 emissions to 1.6 tons per person, whether it is responsible for a lot or a little of the climate change so far.

An international treaty is required to enforce the requirement stated in the report, that CO_2 emissions from the use of energy in industrial production and human consumption would have to fall to at most 1.6 tons a year per person on the planet by midcentury. If this level of emission is too low to be achievable at present, each member of the United Nations can submit its desired amount to the General Assembly as suggested in my proposal presented in Section 9.5. The General Assembly then chooses the median of the submitted amounts as the target to be achieved. To achieve this target, the UN can issue a total number of emission permits equal to the above amount of CO_2 emission per person per year. Nations that have excess numbers of permits are allowed to sell them to the nations in need at prices mutually agreed upon.

After this book was in press, Stern and Bowen (2014) appeared. Its abstract is:

> The year 2015 will be a landmark year for international climate change negotiations. Governments have agreed to adopt a universal legal agreement on climate change at the 21st Conference of Parties (COP21) to the United Nations Framework Convention on Climate Change (UNFCCC) in Paris in 2015. The agreement will come into force no later than 2020.
>
> This book focuses on the prospects for global agreement, how to encourage compliance with any such agreement and perspectives of key players in the negotiations — the United States, India, China, and the EU.

The reader is referred to the above book. While our book, especially Section 9.5, represents the author's view on this topic, it may be of interest to compare Section 9.5 of our book to the discussions in the above reference to find out how the discussion of this topic has evolved.

References

Barrett, Scott. (2009), "The Coming Global Climate — Technology Revolution," *Journal of Economic Perspectives*, 23(2): 53–75.

Stern, Nicholas and Alex Bowen, (2014). *The Global Development of Policy Regimes to Combat Climate Change*. Singapore: World Scientific Publishing Co.

United Nations, 2014. *Report to Control Climate Change.*

Xu, Y., (2011a), "The Use of a Goal for SO_2 Mitigation Planning and Management in China's 11th Five-Year Plan," *Journal of Environmental Planning and Management*, 54(6): 769–783.

Xu, Y., (2011b), "Improvements in the Operation of SO_2 Scrubbers in China's Coal Power Plants," *Environmental Science and Technology*, 45(2): 380–385.

Questions

1. What are possible ways to limit harmful emissions from the use of given energy sources?
2. How can existing technology be improved to reduce the harmful effects on the environment?
3. Name alternative sources of energy to coal and oil. Discuss two sources that will contribute most to improving the environment and are at the time most promising for adoption, and give reasons for your answers.
4. What have China's efforts to protect its environment been?
5. Name the efforts by the US to help improve the environments of other nations.
6. What needs to be done to control carbon emissions in the world?
7. What role can the United Nations play in limiting the amount of carbon emissions in the world?

Index

Adam Smith's "invisible hand", 2, 6–7, 9, 62, 99
air pollution, 3, 8, 17–19, 23, 26, 31, 33–34, 66–67, 77, 81, 84, 121–122, 152, 170
Al Gore, 41, 153
Andreoni and Levison's economic model, 1, 159–162, 166
Article 26 of China's constitution, 23
Asia-Pacific Partnership (APP), 182–183

Bayesian statistics, 104, 114–115
Biofuels, 176–177, 184
   algae, 176–177
   Solix Biofuels plant, 177
Bohigian, David, 182
BP Statistical Review, 180
Brock–Mirman model of economic growth, 87–88
Bush, George W., 182
Business As Usual (BAU) scenario, 150

cap and trade, 154
CAPM model in finance, 130
carbon capture and storage (CCS), 171, 184
   strategies for storing emitted carbon, 171
central planner, 3, 61–63, 73, 75–76, 81, 83, 88, 96, 133, 138–139

certainty equivalent, 97–98, 106
China Country Analysis Brief, 20
China Statistical Yearbook, 66, 141
China's 10th Five-Year Plan, 170
China's 11th Five-Year Plan, 28, 30, 170, 179
China's constitution, Article 26, 23
China's laws and agencies for environmental protection
   Air Pollution Prevention and Control Law of 1987, 23
   China's Cleaner Production Promotion Law, 23–24
   Energy Conservation Law of 1997, 23, 30–31
   Environmental Protection Law for Trial Implementation, 23
   Solid Waste Law of 1995, 23
   Water Pollution Prevention and Control Law of 1984, 23
   Water and Soil Conservation Law of 1991, 23
China's coal-fired power sector, 22, 25, 171–172, 181
China's electricity generation, 19, 28–29, 179
China's emission intensity, 22
China's energy consumption, 18, 20, 24, 29
China's energy–environment problem, 18–23
   air pollution, 18–19

emission of CO_2, 21–23
energy supply, 20–21
water pollution, 19
China's development, major
directions in
    market reform, 35
    democratic government, 35
China's environment protection,
two major aspects of the
problem, 32–33
China's hydropower, 28–29,
179–180
China's incentive schemes, 8, 18,
25–28, 31, 34, 143, 151, 170, 175,
178
China's investment in cleaner
plants, 171
China's macroeconomy (*includes*
Chinese macroeconomy), 61–62,
81, 83–85
China's major hindrance to
environmental law enforcement,
30, 32
China's Ministry of Environment
Protection, 34, 170
China's National Climate Change
Program, 180
China's plans for five nuclear
power stations, 38–39, 176
    AP 1000 technologies, 38
China's policies for environmental
protection, 25–26
    imposition of large fines on
    pollutant emissions, 26
    "polluter pays" system, 26
    reducing amount of sulphur
    dioxide, 25–26
    reducing the use of coal, 25–26
    tax structure to benefit
    environment, 26

technologies to treat
    wastewater, prevent air
    pollution, 26
China's policies for reducing CO_2
emission, 26–28
China's Renewable Energy Law,
175
China's State Environmental
Protection Administration
(SEPA), 23–24
China's target of reducing energy
consumption, 24, 30
    Wen Jiabao's policy
    statements for
    environmental protection,
    24–25, 29–30
China's Three Gorges Dam, 29,
175, 180
China's greenhouse gas (GHG)
emissions, 21, 29, 172, 180–181
China's wind energy, 175, 181
China's wind resources, 28
Chow's proposal for carbon
emission reduction, 153–154
Clean Development Mechanism
(CDM), 28, 180
clean energy, 8, 15, 22, 30–31, 37,
52, 169, 177–179, 183
clean energy, use of, 169
CO_2 emission, finding an optimum
path of, 12, 42–44, 50–58,
    illustrative numerical
    solutions, 55
    Socolow and Lam's optimum
    path, 56–57
CO_2 emission policy, four
parameters for the optimum, 11,
120
CO_2 total level in the atmosphere,
22

Cobb–Douglas production
function, 4, 62–63, 76, 80, 96,
120, 150
common but differentiated
responsibilities, 27
Constant Relative Risk Aversion
(CRRA) utility function, 112
utility function, 10, 45, 139,
160–161
    cost and benefit of pollution, 4
    linear utility function, 160
    optimal path for
        CO_2emission, 11, 13, 44
    parametric utility functions,
        43
    player's utility function, 13
consumption and production, 3,
17–18, 72
consumption goods, 4, 88, 160
continuous time, 12, 50, 106, 108
control theory, 49
controlling pollution (*includes*
reducing pollution), 5, 9, 23, 31,
65, 143, 146, 151, 169–170, 173
cost of monitoring, 35
critical evaluations of evidence
supporting the EKC, 165–166
cross-section regressions, 129–130
cross-section EKC regressions, 165

deterministic model, 50, 89, 93
developed nations on climate
change, 27, 117–119, 182
developing nations on climate
change, 117–119, 182
discount rate for mitigating
climate change, 103–104,
106–107, 147
discrete time, 12, 50, 96, 106, 148
dynamic constraint, 13, 44, 73, 86,
89, 93, 119, 134, 138–139

dynamic game model, 3, 11, 13–14,
58, 117–118
dynamic optimization problem,
12–13, 42–44, 49–52, 54, 58, 83,
88, 91, 96, 100, 118, 133, 146

econometric analysis, 83, 141
econometric model, 99–101
econometric problems, 127,
163–164
    unit root and spurious
        correlation, 127
    testing for unit roots,127–128
    heteroskedicity, 128
    breaking points, 128
    simultaneous-equations bias,
        128–129
economic analysis of emission
permits, 144
    static analysis, 144–146
    dynamic analysis, 144,
        146–147
    general equilibrium analysis,
        144, 147
    regulation of carbon emission,
        119, 144, 152
Economy and Lieberthal's
proposal, 31–32
efficiency of American coal-fired
plants, 171–172, 181–182
efficient allocation of resources,
1–2, 7, 62
    marginal product, 1
emission permits, 3, 5–10, 14,
33–35, 73–76, 83–84, 139,
143–149, 151, 152, 154–156, 157,
185
    economic and political issues,
    157
    emission permits, revising the
    distribution, 155

emission permits, use of, 33,
157–158,
China's per capita emission,
157–158
empirical relation between
pollution and GDP, 84, 163
increase in air pollution, 84
increase in China's
construction activities, 85
unanticipated increase in
money supply, 84
environmental economics, 2–14,
32–33, 166
environmental Kuznets curve by
Andreoni and Levinson, 160–161
environmental Kuznets curve
(EKC), 1, 15, 123, 125–130,
159–166
equalization of the marginal costs,
144
estimation of production function
with energy as input, 135–136
EU-ETS (European Union
Emission Trading Scheme),
148–149
examining China's policies for
environmental protection, 25–26
reducing amount of sulphur
dioxide, 25–26
reducing the use of coal, 25–26
"polluter pays" system, 26
imposition of large fines on
pollutant emissions, 26
tax structure to benefit
environment, 26
technologies to treat
wastewater, prevent air
pollution, 26
externality, 7, 144

factors of production, 2, 120, 137
physical capital, 2, 4, 42, 44,
75, 135, 139, 144
labor, 2, 4, 42, 44, 62, 71,
73–75, 94, 120, 135, 139,
144–145
factors that hinder enforcement of
China's environmental laws, 30
factors to help implementation of
laws and policies for China's
environment, 31
fixed effect model, 127, 136
free market, 31
Fukushima accident, 23, 176
fusion power, 176

G8 summit, 27
game theory, 14, 120
genetically engineered
carbon-eating trees, 153
global warming, 11–12, 14, 17–18,
27, 41–42, 44, 52, 58, 87–88,
91–93, 95, 98–100, 103–105, 107,
109, 113–114, 120, 153, 155,
172–173, 181
Great Leap Forward and the
Cultural Revolution, 80
Green GDP, 5, 10, 61, 65, 73, 77,
81, 84
Green Jobs and Clean Energy
Economy Report, 178–179
greenhouse gas emissions, 21, 27,
29, 41, 150, 172, 176, 180–182

Hu Jintao, 27
hydropower, 28–29, 179–180,

incentives, 8, 151
economic incentives, 18,
25–26, 31, 143, 170, 175, 178
market incentives, 22, 31

industrial air pollution among Chinese Provinces, model for, 122–123
Industrial Revolution, 22, 27, 153
inertia of change, 43, 50, 53
Integrated Assessment Models (IAMs) for climate change, 115
Intergovernmental Panel on Climate Change, 22
International Energy Agency (IEA), 21, 164

joint density, 111

Kuznets, Simon, 159
Kyoto Protocol, 21, 23, 27–28, 41

Lagrange multiplier, 6, 12–13, 45–46, 63, 89, 94, 108
Lagrangean expression, 6, 44, 49–50, 53, 74, 96, 139
Lake Taihu, 19
level of total CO_2 in the atmosphere, 22
Light emitting diodes (LEDs), 172–173
linear-quadratic optimum control problem, 45

macroeconomic data of China, 62, 66, 69, 72
macroeconomic model for uncertain effect of pollution, 96–98, 100
macroeconomic model's purpose, 62
macroeconomic models assuming optimization, 62–66
  market solution, 73–76
  China's pollution, 76–83

macroeconomic models for pollution, 61
  economic implications, 64–65
Major Economies Process (MEP), 182
market economy, 2, 61–62, 73, 75, 139
market equilibrium, 144
market failure, 7, 61–62, 75, 81, 83–84
market reform, 35
matrix Ricatti equations, 49–50
maximization of expected utility, theory of, 104
measuring change of utility, 72–73
method of ordinary least squares regression, 126, 129
methods to control pollution
  command and control, 143
  economic incentives, 143
mitigating climate change, 104–106
mitigation of global warming, 109
model to explain the increase in China's air pollution, 84–85
model to mitigate effect of climate change, 87–92
model of Socolow and Lam, 42–43

nanocatalysts, 173
Nash equilibrium, 11, 13, 118, 120–121
National Leading Group for Dealing with Climate Change, 180
natural capital, 2–3, 7, 149
natural gas (includes shale gas), 173
New York Times, 171–172
Nordhaus and Boyer's economic model, 1, 87, 93, 95
normative economics, 62
nuclear power plants, 176

nuclear power, share in China's
electricity generation, 29
null hypothesis, 128–130, 162–164

Obama administration, 172
one-tail test, 126–127
optimal control, 12, 42–43, 46,
49–50, 52, 89, 91, 96
optimization model, purpose of,
98–99
ordinary regression model, 125
Organization for Economic
Co-operation and Development
(OECD), 21

panel data regression model,
125–126
Pareto optimum, 144–149
parametric analysis, 43
permission permits, 10, 33, 35
permission permits proposal, 34–36
pollutant discharge in China, 24,
26
pollution and rate of consumption
growth, model for, 133–135
pollution differences in China's
provinces, model for, 121, 147
Pontryagen maximum principle,
50, 108
prediction by Malthus, 52
price of air pollution permits, 81
private ownership of natural
resources, 10
probability distribution, 103
problem of maximization, 6, 45,
61, 93–94, 104, 108
problems in US in defining
renewable energy, 177–178
property rights, 3, 6, 8–10, 33, 84,
157
protection of environment, model
for, 138–139

quantitative measurement,
113–114

Ramsey growth model, 107
rate of relative risk aversion, 109
real GDP, 66, 81, 83, 122–127, 130,
135, 163, 165
reducing annual CO_2 emission, 42
reducing the rate of increase of
carbon emission, 22
regressions to explain
consumption, 70

SO_2 scrubbers, 169–170
desulfurized electricity price
premium, 170
solar energy, 174
solar photovoltaic (PV)
panels, 174–175
solutions to China's energy and
environmental degradation,
17–18
specific utility functions, 43
Stackelberg solution, 13
statistical analysis, 112–113
statistical testing of
Andreoni–Levinson EKC,
161–162
statistical testing of one version of
the EKC, 162–164
stochastic discount factor, 109,
112–113, 115

technological innovations in the
production of clean energy, 22
technology of scrubbing, 86
Three Gorges Dam project, 29
Tools to analyze four types of
economic models, 14
t-test, 127–130, 163–165
two-person game, 10–11

ultra-supercritical technology,
181–182
UN Climate Change Conference,
41, 57, 183
Copenhagen Accord, 41
uncertainty, 8, 14, 58, 87, 96–98,
103–104, 106–107, 109–110, 115
United Nations Framework
Convention on Climate Change,
21
United Nations, role in controlling
CO_2 emissions, 169, 183–184
US clean-energy trade mission to
China, 182
US per-capita emission, 154–155
US Sulfur Dioxide Trading
System, 148
utility function, 4–5, 8–11, 13,
43–45, 49–54, 56–58, 61, 63–65,
70–71, 73, 75–77, 81, 83–84, 93,
95–96, 98–99, 103, 105–106, 110,
113, 120, 122, 133, 139, 160–161

water pollution among different
Chinese provinces, model for,
121–122
Weitzman, Martin, 111–113, 115
Wen Jiabao, 24, 29
wind energy, 175, 181
World Development Indicators
(WDI), 164
World Health Organization
(WHO), 18

Yangtze River, 19, 26
Yellow River, 19

Zhu Rongji, 32

Printed in the United States
By Bookmasters